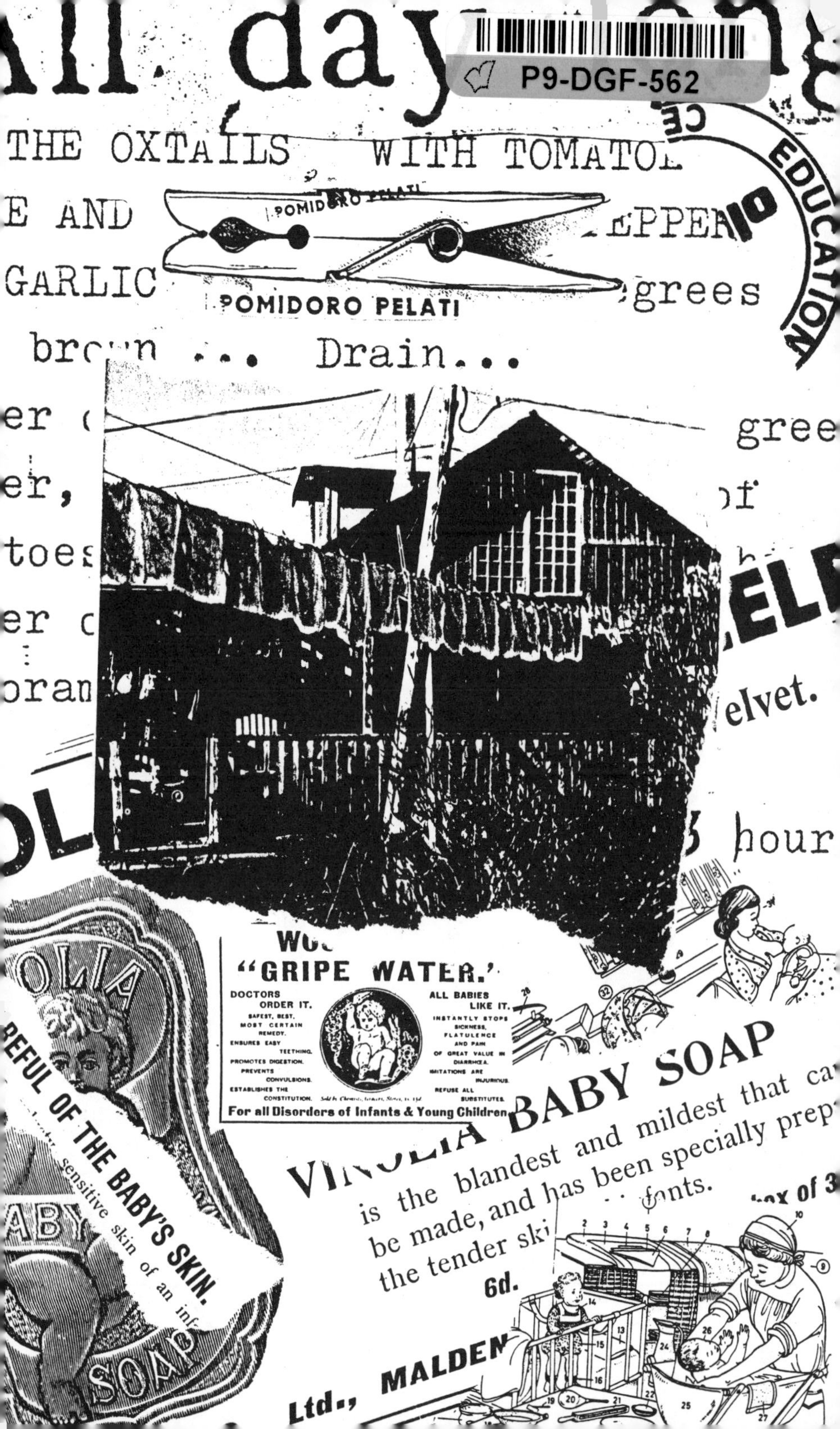
All day
P9-DGF-562
THE OXTAILS WITH TOMATO
E AND
GARLIC
POMIDORO PELATI
POMIDORO PELATI
EPPER
grees
EDUCATION
brown ... Drain...
er
gree
er,
of
toes
er
ELE
elvet.
hour
"GRIPE WATER."
DOCTORS ORDER IT.
SAFEST, BEST, MOST CERTAIN REMEDY.
ENSURES EASY TEETHING.
PROMOTES DIGESTION.
PREVENTS CONVULSIONS.
ESTABLISHES THE CONSTITUTION.
ALL BABIES LIKE IT.
INSTANTLY STOPS SICKNESS, FLATULENCE AND PAIN
OF GREAT VALUE IN DIARRHŒA.
IMITATIONS ARE INJURIOUS.
REFUSE ALL SUBSTITUTES.
For all Disorders of Infants & Young Children.
OLIA
REFUL OF THE BABY'S SKIN.
sensitive skin of an inf
ABY
SOAP
VINOLIA BABY SOAP
is the blandest and mildest that ca
be made, and has been specially prep
the tender ski
fants.
6d.
Ltd., MALDEN

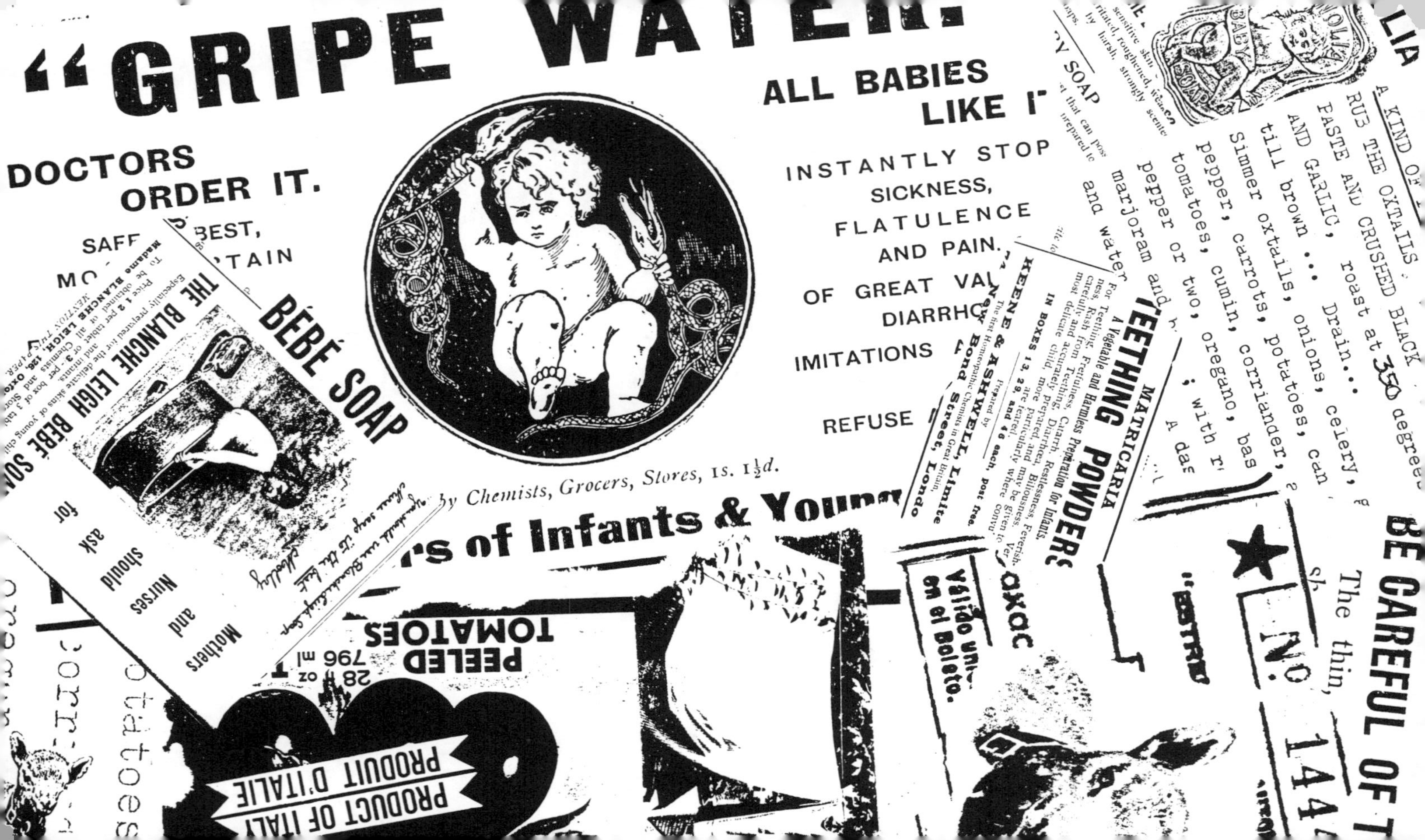
"GRIPE WATER"
ALL BABIES LIKE I
DOCTORS ORDER IT.
INSTANTLY STOP
SICKNESS,
FLATULENCE
AND PAIN.
OF GREAT VAL
DIARRH
IMITATIONS
REFUSE
by Chemists, Grocers, Stores, 1s. 1½d.
s of Infants & Young
SAFF
BEST,
TAIN
BÉBÉ SOAP
THE BLANCHE LEIGH BÉBÉ SOA
Especially prepared for the delicate skins of young chi and infants.
Price 1 2 per tablet or 3 per box of 3 tab
To be obtained of all Chemists and Sto
Madame BLANCHE LEIGH, 126, Oxfo
You should use Blanche Leigh Soap
Nurses says it's the best
Molly
Mothers and Nurses should ask for
MATRICARIA
TEETHING POWDERS
A Vegetable and Harmless Preparation for Infants.
For Teething, Fretfulness, Catarrh, Restlessness, Feverishness, Rash from Teething, Diarrhœa, Biliousness. Ver carefully and accurately prepared, and may be given to most delicate child, more particularly where convu are feared.
IN BOXES 13, 29, and 46 each, post free.
Prepared by
KEENE & ASHWELL, Limite
The first Homoeopathic Chemists in Great Britain,
New Bond Street, Londo
A KIND OF
RUB THE OXTAILS
PASTE AND CRUSHED BLACK
AND GARLIC, roast at 350 degrees
till brown ... Drain...
Simmer oxtails, onions, celery,
pepper, carrots, potatoes, can
tomatoes, cumin, corriander,
pepper or two, oregano, bas
marjoram and ; with
and water A das
BABY
SOAP
sensitive skin
ritated, roughened,
by harsh, strongly scente
Y SOAP
that can poss
prepared to
BE CAREFUL OF T
The thin,
No 1444
"ESTRE
axac
Válido uni
en el Boleto.
PEELED TOMATOES
28 fl oz
796 ml
PRODUCT OF ITALY
PRODUIT D'ITALIE
otatoes
corri

Mothers Talk Back

Mothers Talk Back

Momz Radio

Edited by Margaret Dragu,
Sarah Sheard,
and Susan Swan

Coach House Press
Toronto

Thanks to the Momz Radio Collective from the 'Momz Radio Show' Series: Renee Rodin, Izabel Martinez, Maxine Young, Hilde Westerkamp, Pat Salter, Susan Smyth, Gay Zimmerman, Jan Kudelka, Pearl Hunt, Luke Hunt, Cindi Mellon, Libby Scheier, Dr. K. Emmott, Catherine MacLeod, Lyn Flitton, Chris Morton, Dora Penzon, Clarita Blanco, A. Ellen Dragu, Loretta Hewison, Sarah Sheard, Catherine Hahn, Paul Gibbons, Dr. Robert Baker, Jim Munro, Tsuneko Kokubo, Mona Fertig, Judith Hoffman, Wendi Gilson, Joanne Arnott. Thanks also to Jane Ellison, Patrick Ready, Lisa Jo Osland, Camilla Mason, Jill Gamley, David Barsamian, Bob McKelvie, Diane Martin, Gillian Morton and Pat Cates.

Published with the assistance of the Canada Council and the Ontario Arts Council. The radio program 'Momz Radio' was originally funded by the Explorations Program of the Canada Council.

Canadian Cataloguing in Publication Data

Mothers talk back

ISBN 0-88910-420-4

1. Mothers.   I. Dragu, Margaret.   II. Sheard, Sarah.   III. Swan, Susan.

HQ759.M65 1991   306.874'3   C91-094971-9

Contents

Introduction

Becoming a mother was to step through a door I imagined would be as familiar as my own past—after all, I was a child once, had observed my own mother, other mothers with children—but if I had known the transformation that awaited me, I'm not sure I'd have taken that first step.

I was shocked and depressed after my baby came, sure there was something wrong with me, that my confused, unmaternal, helpless fear was perverse, sick, bad. I remember spending a lot of time rocking myself and my baby in a borrowed, one-armed rocking chair. Did it rain every day, or was it just my imagination? Jim was away working in the furniture factory where he had recently nearly lost a finger. On a tight budget, isolated with a semi-rural case of cabin fever, no electricity, I rationed propane for hot water—and the nine-volt batteries for the radio, my big joy. I would cry when the batteries died while preparing my daughter's dinner bottle of formula.

My baby was born sickly, requiring frequent hospitalization. I didn't believe the experts when they told me it hadn't been my fault, although during pregnancy I had avoided coffee, liquor, drugs, even tea, except herbal. I'd taken my vitamins, done only low-impact aerobics. Was I being punished for my ambivalence? I hadn't been sure I really wanted a baby, unlike my girlfriends who were still single and noting the biological *tick tock* with despair. For me, pregnancy was a deeply mystical force I'd been ineffective at warding off. My other friends had children in their teens or twenties. How had they done it? Why were their kids so great, and how did they cope, and how did they get from there to here?

Dysfunctional was the term in vogue for women with feelings like mine.

Ah, the joy. The pain of joy. To be forced to love someone who would only grow up to leave me. To love and know someone who was so innocent and good and for whom I was completely responsible. The telephone became another lifeline: to doctors, to friends. Maxine, drawing on her England-during-the-Blitz experience, helped me cope with no electricity. I could keep a formula bottle cool by wrapping it in layers of newspapers. Renee talked me down, allowing me to feel scary feelings—anger, frustration, indignation. And Jane—my only childless buddy, who stuck with me as I de-glamorized, de-single-ized, and turned into Wilma Flintstone, a.k.a. Momma Bear.

Those first four horrible months, my head began to fill with voices, as if I were a kind of mad radio program crammed full of Noam Chomsky, Oldie Goldie Platter Spinners, Rosie's traffic report, 'Morningside,' 'Union Made from Co-op,' right-wing Nashville C&W, Chicks-on-Sticks bubble gum, AM ski reports, Larry King, new wave, new jazz, new age, letters from my girlfriends, advice, recipes, home remedies, tears, hugs.

Was I drowning or was I waving?

Letters, telephone lines, and radio waves in my brain kept me afloat: *SOS. SOS. You are tuned to Momz Radio. Esta es Radio Mamasita. Ici Radio Maman, bonjour!*

My friend, Adah, asked me, 'Where did that single life go?' Who was this exhausted, fat, miserable shrew who spent all her time now in playgrounds, or cooking, shopping, cleaning, wiping up poop, worrying, rocking, soothing? I was so tired, grey-haired suddenly, with time for nothing except child care, and on top of that, I was invisible. So normal, I was just a statistic. People walked right over me, my baby, the stroller, the diaper bag. Michele Landsberg wrote: 'Women and children, last.' Why hadn't I seen this before? What planet was I living on? Oh, right. The 'single' planet. The land of time and the luxury of being alone.

Becoming a mom provided immediate entry into Feminism 403. The emotional and historical barnacles encrusting the role of mother were shocking. I was an accomplice in my own oppression at home. My experience of parenting *was* different from a man's, and I resented being punished for it. I was—and still am—looking for a part-time job where I could combine child care and working. Why was this so hard? All the magazines that talked about the revolution in the workplace—new skills, new attitudes, job-sharing, daycare on worksite—on what planet did it exist? The anthropomorphic world of children, of *Babar, Curious George, Dr. Seuss,* Ladybird picture books, Robert Munch, Beatrix Potter, 'Sesame Street' and Mickey Mouse was exquisite and yet, as a society, we seemed to hate animals and children. We were exterminating whole species daily and pushing a growing number of children below the poverty line in the battle zones of abuse, war, violence, dwindling resources, and rationed love. We sentimentalized mothers, children, and animals while doing systemic violence to them.

I felt angry.

But I turned on. I wrote, performed, made art—barely—inside tiny windows of opportunity. Jan Kudelka kept three typewriters around her house so she could type a line or two of her playscript while tending both her pre-school-aged children.

Susan Swan testified, on Erika Ritter's radio show: 'Single mom, writer ... Yup, something had to go, and at times it did—the writing.'

I wondered if I would survive, so tired and impatient, worrying whether I'd kill my child, flee my partner, escape to Morocco, the South Pacific. There was no place for an abandoning mother to go. Men walked out on their kids, unpunished. Or stayed to become domesticated—caught, caged up with women and children. How many abandoning mothers did anyone know?

It was easy to leave it all to mom, because mom picked up his socks when he was a kid but made his sister pick up her own. 'Real' commitment to work and success was defined as one foot on the corporate ladder and the other in a cardiac-arrest unit. Because a baby was of mother born and suckled by her, and she was so busy, she looked like she knew what she was doing.

I didn't know what I was doing. Why was I expected to be an instant expert at motherhood skills?

By the time my daughter was a year old, I was determined to do something with the voices filling my head. I successfully applied for a Canada Council Explorations Grant to do a series of interviews, writings, lullabies—in different languages, with music—by, for, and about moms. I interviewed nine moms, solicited moms' writing from across Canada and in some parts of the U.S.A. Well-meaning Bible thumpers sent me psalms and prayers. Baby-product catalogues arrived. Eventually I got 75 responses from fabulous women who were moms: poems, journals, recipes, anecdotes, essays—handwritten, typewritten, word-processed or scribbled on napkins—some very professional, inquiring about payment and copyright, some sad and shocking, all passionate, true-life stuff. 'Momz Radio' gave women permission to cut the crap about motherhood. Mostly poor women, but not all, unsentimentally shattered the mommy myths of eternal sacrifice, eternal niceness, eternally perfect nurturer, and identified mommy work as being hard, invisible, unpaid, saddling women with enormous cultural/political/ spiritual expectations, double-sided morality, judgment. The enormous changes, physically, emotionally, that motherhood brought to women of every class, creed, nationality, income, age, were shared and acknowledged publicly at last.

My daughter Aretha is now two and a half. She makes jokes and kisses my ow-ies better and is a terrific hugger and a great kisser, and we can sing and dance, play the castanets and wave pink flags, laugh and cry and love each other enormously. My daughter has won me over. Dragged me kicking and screaming through the door into motherhood.

But without the other mothers in my life who revealed themselves so unstintingly to me and who, in turn, helped me to reveal myself, I would not be as strong and accepting of my motherhood as I am today. It is to them and to moms everywhere that I have dedicated this book.

— *Margaret Dragu*

P.S. from Susan Swan and Sarah Sheard

Speaking of conceptions, this book began, initially, out of love and affection for Margaret Dragu, dear friend and fellow mother. As the interviews came in, though, we began to recognize bits of ourselves in each of them and became aware that, while Swan and I were both writers, neither of us had yet addressed our own experiences as mothers in our work. Swan referred to the schizophrenia that characterized managing her relationship to both in her life, and I felt a lingering self-consciousness at sharing private observations of the most profound relationship I'd known, worried I'd be judged guilty of indulgent sentimentality, banality, or of being repellently clinical. I cannot yet bring myself to fictionalize that part of my life. Yet, we became more and more moved by an urgency to help crack open these roles, admit light into them, claim the truth of this experience for ourselves and bring the perception of motherhood as it was actually being lived by women around us into truer alignment with reality, instead of the fantastical versions in such persistent circulation today—for the sakes of the sons and daughters we are raising, as much as for ourselves. It is hoped that this book will be only one of many occasions in which women course-correct the institution of motherhood, banish something of the schizophrenia and self-consciousness that so many of us feel about our own experience. Diane Martin joined forces with us on this book, interviewing and transcribing, for love and no money, like the rest of us engaged in real mothers' work.

— *Sarah Sheard*

Beyond Ambivalence

Premature Baby, Premature Mom

Margaret Dragu, born in 1953 in Regina, Saskatchewan
Mother of Rhea
Interviewed by Renee Rodin

RENEE Can you tell us about bringing your daughter home from the hospital?

MARGARET First let me tell you about a dream I had recently. I was in labour, knowing that I was only two-months pregnant, and giving birth to a strange kind of doll's head that was still quite wrinkled. It still looked very much like a baby's head, but it was just a head, and that was all. Because it was so early, only the head had formed, but the head could talk and cry, and it was like a vaguely normal baby. I felt terrified that this out-of-control birth was going on, and it was too soon, and this tiny, fragile head had to be taken care of.

RENEE How does the dream relate to your experience with Aretha?

MARGARET Aretha was a premature baby—one month early—and I remember now clearly that there was no time to feel anything about it, because she was born early, and she was sort of sick, and she needed all this care, and we couldn't seem to get out of the hospital, and everything seemed very out of control. Then we went home, and she was still sick, and we had to keep going to the hospital every day, and then eventually go into the hospital and stay for another week. I slept in the hospital. It was like being on the Starship Enterprise, with these voices talking and doctors being called in and lights going on and treatments—just this endless hospital kind of thing that never seemed to stop.

RENEE You are shaking your head when you are talking. Do you think maybe the head was you? The baby was out of your body, and you had to deal with your mind more than anything else?

MARGARET Maybe I had to control my thoughts because I

couldn't allow myself to feel anything. The feelings would occasionally rush up, but I had to keep everything in the head. I couldn't experience anything. I had real trouble breast-feeding, and it was an emotional problem for me. I felt a lot of guilt round it not working. I think I was so frightened and tense, I could have turned off the taps. Maybe I didn't want to accept any help because it was like a chink in the armour, and if I accepted any help, it would all come tumbling down. I think I pulled everything in for a sense of control and felt like I was coping really well, but I don't think I probably was at all. It's not my fault I was having trouble breast-feeding, but it made me feel that I was bad—and this feeling may be one of the by-products of having no sense of control.

I remember when we were leaving the hospital the first time and the test came back, and we still had to stay. I was surrounded by women who would give birth, they would arrive in the middle of the night, and the baby would be there, and they would be there for a day or two, and they would be very happy, and they would leave. I was surrounded by a huge cast—like an English play that was going on—the other actors were all quickly passing through, but I could never leave. In the ward, we had only those thin muslin curtains around us. If you wanted to cry or yell, you would disturb everybody, so you had to keep everything extremely contained. There was no privacy. Everybody was really nice to me, but I didn't know what a normal birth was like, or what I should be doing. It was another blow to my confidence. In order for Aretha to be alright, it seemed as if I had to block off all my instincts and my feelings about everything, or I would have just died on the spot.

RENEE This was a survival mechanism?

MARGARET It took a long time for that to peel away. The next thing I remember was that Jim was working, and I was with the baby at home, and I was very depressed and in a kind of strange fog. I remember wondering when I would turn into a mother. It seemed like I was there, and there was the baby, but I just didn't have any feelings—it seemed abstract.

RENEE There is a myth that, when you have the baby, you are going to be the total mother—but it's a process, it takes a long time, and people don't tell you this. People don't talk about the negative side of having babies. There is the myth that you are going to be a great mother immediately, and have all the feelings—and you have gone through an incredible, traumatic experience, and your chemicals are going nuts, and you are suddenly coping with a human who has been in your body for nine months, and it takes a long time. How old is Aretha now?

MARGARET A year and a half.

RENEE I think you are just starting to tap in to what actually happened.

MARGARET I am just starting to remember the feelings. That's what the dreams are about. I feel a lot better. One day, Jim was working, and I was rocking in the rocking chair, and I was thinking about what I would feel like if he were killed in a car crash—this is still a fantasy that comes and goes. I fantasized that Aretha was killed in a car crash with him. I couldn't get this thought out of my head—of them both dying—and I spent two or three days just sitting in that chair, rocking back and forth, holding the baby and crying. After I had finished that, I realized that I would be really sad if they were both dead. I turned around and looked at her for the first time and saw that this baby wasn't an it, and that it was a baby girl, and that she was still there, and that I was still there, and he was still there, and that I would miss them. I was strongly attached to them. I had to admit that I was strongly attached to them. That was the big breakthrough. I don't know how old she was then—four months?—but it took a long time to get that far.

I remember seeing women in the hospital, they had little layettes, and they would hold their healthy little babies and cuddle them and lay in bed with them. My baby was nearly unconscious, so I couldn't really get it together to pick her up and hold her all the time, she wasn't awake. She was sort of green on top of that—green-orange. I was the healthiest of anybody there, because I didn't have stitches or anything. I would be lying in bed, and everybody would be asking for rooming-in, and I didn't know why they wanted to. What did you do with this lump anyway? It all seemed so extremely mysterious. But the rocking chair episode helped. And then Jim helped a lot, because he is very maternal, very good with her.

RENEE What do you consider are the differences between mothering and fathering?

MARGARET I have the idea from my own childhood that they are really separated—that father is mysterious, and not there, and authoritative, and to be avoided, and mother takes care of you and copes under this patriarchal threat. Jim isn't any of those things that I remember from my childhood, and when I needed help as a mother in knowing what to do—and I still do this—I look and see how he is with her, and it makes such sense to me, and he seems very maternal, he just enjoys her. He plays with her in a really nice way and listens to her and reflects herself back to her in a really spontaneous way. He turns into a gentle kind of clown when they play. It's really wonderful.

I didn't know how to play with her. I often take my cues from him, because it takes me a while to respond to her as she develops to a new stage. I will keep on doing something that worked before—at this age they change so quickly—and I see that he is doing some new developmental thing and it is so wonderful, and so I often take cues from him, because he is so sensitive to what is happening with her. He takes care of her as much as I do, and he feeds her as much as I do and spends as many hours with her as I do and doesn't go away to work. I work at home, and I am temporarily the wage earner at the moment, so he is with her a lot. It is so different from my neighbour down the street. For a long time my neighbour took care of her little boy from seven in the morning until nine at night all by herself. The absent father. Jim's always there, so I just sort of assume he must be a mother! But he is the father!

RENEE Did you want to be pregnant?

MARGARET No. It was an accident. I've had lots of accidents before and had abortions, but this time we decided to have a child, even though I was ambivalent. Part of me wanted strongly to have a baby. I began to think about it, and it began to enter my life as something I wanted, but I didn't make any concrete plans to carry it out. Once I make a decision about something, I usually have a way of making it happen. It's usually very direct. If I am going to clean house, I make a list and do it. If I am going to move somewhere, then I make the reservation and go there. If you want to get something done, then you apply a certain kind of energy to it, and that's how I always make changes. I've made lots of big changes in my life, but the way I made this change in my life seemed to me much more complex, and only part of my brain seemed to know that I was making plans to have this baby. I never had a real sense of possibility or interest in having a baby when I was pregnant before. Because of my relationship with Jim and my sense of my changing life, having a baby seemed to be part of the palette of new colours, but only with part of my brain. The first couple of months of being pregnant were very anxiety-producing.

RENEE How did you finally make the decision to stay pregnant?

MARGARET I'm not sure. Again, it was circumstance. We were waiting, and I was possessed by difficult dreams of giving birth to goats and all those typical weird pregnant dreams, and I would be worried about having a baby and then be so terribly confused. Jim talked to his doctor, who was a family friend and was patient and reassuring, but leaving all possibilities open. We kept talking and leaving it open as a possibility; we kept waiting. Jim was working on an art show at the time; he was working very hard, and I was his secretary. He gave a performance, and I remember him getting in a psychic state in the performance and crying out like a baby, as if this baby was calling out to us through his performance. He remembers this. Then he got a bit tipsy after the opening—I gave him a bottle of brandy to drink before the performance—and afterwards he went out with friends and told them all that I was pregnant. Not meaning, necessarily, that I was going to have a baby, but that he just had to let it out, I think. It was obviously a big topic that we were talking a lot about at the time.

We got one or two phone calls of congratulations the next day, while he was hung over and I was exhausted, which made us feel even more like we had taken steps, but only part of our minds had taken the steps. This ambivalence continued until about a day or so after that. I was taking a bath. I got out of the bathtub, and he said, 'Well, let's do it.' And I said, 'Let's do it.' We had a big kiss, and that was that—we had finally, in a very low-key way, come to decide.

RENEE Had he not wanted you to stay pregnant, would you have stayed pregnant?

MARGARET Hard to say. It was such a confusing time. I didn't seem to be operating with any logic. I would be borrowing from my logic now to say something about then. I probably wouldn't have. I just desperately needed help in making that decision—or I would have made it earlier, I suppose. I wouldn't have dragged out that ambivalence for so long. But ambivalence was something I felt very guilty about and it took a long time to get rid of, for it to go away.

RENEE You mean that you almost didn't have her?

MARGARET Yes, and I would feel guilty that she came early and was sick, and that I was being punished or she was being punished because of me. It must have come from the ancient Christian guilt we were taught as children. Who knows, maybe it was true. Or maybe I was having trouble breast-feeding because I was ambivalent. All the things it's normal to torture yourself with.

RENEE Is it?

MARGARET I think it's natural to torture yourself with guilty thoughts. I think we are taught those things as part of our logic system. Certainly part of the logic system that I have been given. I can choose not to believe it, but I need help in choosing not to believe it. I need alternatives to it.

RENEE Some people believe in the goddess or the god. Some people have a superstructure of belief so that they do not take on all these things. They allow destiny, or fate, or whatever you call it, to be responsible for what happens—that in fact we are not totally in control of our lives and our babies' lives. There are other choices.

MARGARET I would love that. It's hard. It's like an idea with a new root that needs so much attention to keep it growing. I would love to be a Buddhist. It seems to make so much sense to me, but I would have to eschew the culture and the values that I have been given and consciously go over to another one that is quite foreign.

RENEE Now that the tiny green thing is a beautiful, big, healthy, wonderful baby, do you feel responsible for that too? Do you feel that that is because of you?

MARGARET She is partly wonderful because of me. She is partly wonderful because of herself. I think she has an innate energy and is an innate being. She is obviously a separate person, and she has a great sense of humour and is very happy and loves to laugh and is a wonderful person. After the rocking-chair episode, I decided that she was really great, and I loved her. I did write journals on and off during some of those periods of time—which helped me a lot, through just the intensity of feeling and the depression and the changes and stuff—but once things got better, I also got a different kind of busy with her and don't write in the journals quite as much. Also, I have started working again, and there is only so much time—I still jot the odd thing down. But the journal saved my life during the real tough period.

RENEE Because you were able to express yourself in a different way?

MARGARET I couldn't express what I was feeling. My journals were completely pragmatic and would be really boring to anybody but me. I would write complete detailed lists of exactly when she ate and what she ate when she was breast-feeding and formula feeding, because I felt so out of control, and I still didn't know what I was doing, and I thought, Oh my god, if she dies at least I will have a record of what I did and whether I killed her or not, or it will help, and so it would be, '8:07: 15 minutes left breast; three oz. formula.' I was completely obsessed. It's a good thing I wrote it down, or I would have gone crazy. I am sure I *was* kind of crazy.

RENEE It sounds like you were very anxious.

MARGARET Beyond anxiety into a kind of twilight zone I had never entered before. It was also physically very hard living where we do, on an inland canal near Richmond. I felt isolated. We had no electricity. I can't drive a car.

RENEE Do you realize that most women go through anxiety and depression after they have babies? To one degree or another.

MARGARET Anxiety is something that I am finding out that women experience. I sense it almost viscerally. It is a real elemental state. Even if the children are extremely healthy, and it was a planned pregnancy, and they were quite ecstatic, there is a kind of anxiety that goes with it.

RENEE Aside from the hormones, there is a lack of sleep, so many different changes that contribute to that anxiety.

MARGARET It's obviously intense beyond belief. Some people can enjoy it more than others. Some people survive it and pass through it more quickly than others. It seems to be a passage zone, like the Mists of Avalon, that you have to get through to get to some other point. You have to get through some way or another.

RENEE To tap into the joy and highness of it? At this point are you feeling more in control of what's happening?

MARGARET I am feeling more in control. It changes so much. I always feel that I am lagging behind, so I am always slightly disarmed by what keeps coming up. If Aretha is sick, I am almost crushed beyond belief—she hasn't been sick for months, knock on wood—but I go into a panic when she is sick. It doesn't have anything to do with her, it's to do with my relationship with illness and my relationship with me when I have a cold or with my mother when she was sick. I don't have a healthy attitude towards sickness. I think it shouldn't be such a big deal, and that there shouldn't be so many things attached to being sick. I mean, everybody does get colds and flu occasionally. I really should try and be cooler about it all, and I am aware that I rely on Jim to get me through those points when I am a bit too hysterical.

I am still very hard on myself. I think I could do better, and more. I am still working on being more tolerant, and not losing my temper, although sometimes you can't tell I have lost my temper. There are all these things that I want to be better at, but the best part is, now it doesn't matter to me, or I don't worry as much about how I'm doing.

RENEE Do you take time out from your child?

MARGARET Now that she's older, it's easier to leave her with Jim. He can take care of her as well as I can and is as much mother to her as I am. So now, once or twice a week, I am away for the day, and that helps a lot. Not that I don't love her madly, but being away from her, having that break, makes me a lot more positive.

RENEE Does the absence energize you?

MARGARET The stimulation is important and so is the change. I find a way of coping with the stress of suddenly being a mother and having this little being with all these needs is to establish a routine. She seems to really like the routine. It gives me a sense that I am coping, because I am getting everything done in the routine—it's a tangible thing. I love and hate the routine. Jumping into town for a day to take care of my own needs and to break up the routine is a real shot in the arm in many ways.

RENEE It seems very important as a parent to fulfil your own needs.

MARGARET I think so. Although there is a sense—maybe it comes from TV or old Dickens books—that a mother as a martyr is an okay thing. If you're not a martyr, there is something wrong with you. Your needs don't count, and you should put your needs on hold, and you're bad if you have any needs. Yet there is, at the same time, the other idea, that you should put your kids in daycare, and be a career person, and not worry about their needs at all, or get somebody else to take care of them. There is some kind of double message there. I'm not following that latter one; I find myself more prey to the first one. I feel a bit guilty sometimes that I don't do it better, that I do need other stimulation. I feel guilty that I am a person! I don't know where the idealized version comes from.

RENEE How do you feel about your daughter now?

MARGARET I seem to like her more and more, and she seems more and more interesting to me. I just love it when she laughs and she makes faces and she has jokes. There are things we can do together that are fun. She likes to dance, and likes music, and we have little dance steps that we do, and little running jokes. We are getting to be buddies, and that is great. I don't want to turn into my own mother. I would like to have a better relationship with my mother. I would like to have a better relationship with my daughter. I would like to have a better relationship with the world. I would like to be a better person. What the hell! But I don't think I am damaging Aretha in the process, and at the beginning, I really worried that I would, because it seemed not right, or that I wasn't right.

RENEE It was a weak beginning?

MARGARET It was a tough beginning, and it took a while to come out of that.

RENEE You said before that sometimes when you lose your temper, which you don't like, that no one even realizes you have lost your temper. How does one go about losing one's temper without others knowing?

MARGARET Well, you just get depressed. There is a certain type of depression you can tap into or become ... a kind of grumpy depression that is really a lost temper that nobody knows about.

RENEE So it turns onto yourself again?

MARGARET You just turn it inwards.

RENEE It's anger that doesn't get expressed outwards?

MARGARET An edited anger, I guess. Most of the time it is ridiculous to get angry at a little child who is not doing anything worth your anger, and isn't being bad, and is completely innocent.

RENEE But at times is definitely testing you and is wanting you to show some kind of limit or some kind of emotion.

MARGARET I think the whole issue of limits paralyses most parents and reveals their morality to themselves, and it's shocking to find it. That's when I do remember how I was raised—not only how I was raised, but how my mother was raised and my father was raised. They were both abused a lot. Although I was never physically abused, in trying not to physically abuse me, they still had the same morality attached to it, even though they thought that whipping children was bad. Rural people of that generation were very isolated—they were in communities, but still very isolated. Children died from being corrected. That went with the morality of that kind of fervent Christian, dingbat, lost, rural, anxious life/death. The thirties ... I guess. They weren't isolated incidents, they weren't peculiar, to have been physically abused. That was very common.

RENEE So you weren't abused?

MARGARET In our time, when we were raised, you sort of slapped children and spanked them, and limits were constantly being discussed between parent and child in the small physical way. So it is like ... so slapping and crying and spanking and crying is the way you grew up, right?

When Aretha tests my limits, not only do I remember ... time sort of explodes in on itself—you become a strange witch when you are a mother, you remember ... things aren't so linear, so you can get these feelings. These feelings are not coming from a linear source, necessarily. I can feel generations of experiences, and I don't even know quite what they are sometimes. I feel these things that aren't directly between me and Aretha when she is testing my limits—when she keeps wanting to turn the cold-water tap on and keeps wanting to scrape and move the table, or keeps wanting to bang her shoe on the window and try to break it, and I know she must not—or must not touch the hot stove or she will get burnt.

RENEE Are you afraid to get angry at those times? Are you afraid that you will lose control and maybe become abusive if you get angry?

MARGARET I think I used to be afraid, although I don't feel I would hit her. I have never hit anyone. I have slapped one person once, but that is not how I express myself. I don't see myself as an abusing person, although I can imagine how it happens. I am more tolerant about it. I understand both sides of the coin a little more now, and I see it as being more complex than I used to. That's not what I am worried about as much. I would rather be perfect. I would rather not let it upset me. I would rather distract her. I would rather be like all the great books—like the Penelope Leach books—and turn something negative into something positive very quickly and move on. But I can't necessarily be perfect, in that zone when the limit testing happens. I just have some of these memories, and some of these memories are not necessarily my own, but they are from people who have been attached to me, maybe from people I don't even know. I imagine they are from other generations of people who are attached to me through my family unit. People who I would very easily have not bothered thinking about ever again. I had detached myself from my family very successfully. I still have, relatively, but that detachment was threatened, not just by them, but by myself in having a baby. I was very surprised to feel that. The reconnection despite myself. I don't, for example, spend any more time with my mother than I ever did, but I think about her a lot more than I ever did. I think I have managed to kind of jolly our position together into a fairly positive one, even though we don't see each other very often. I have manoeuvred it in a very adult way to this kind of level. But all these things have been brought up again—and I find that I have very passionate feelings, many not so positive, that I had put away—and I resent the fact that I have to plough through all these again.

Performance Anxiety
The Breast-Feeding Nightmare

Gloria Hershorn, born in 1950 in Toronto, Ontario
Mother of Rosie
Interviewed by Margaret Dragu

MARGARET When did you first want to have a baby?

GLORIA When I was about two, as far as I remember, but I always thought I would wait until I grew up. Then I suddenly realized that I was never going to grow up, and I was going to get too old, so I started trying in earnest when I was about 35 years old. I actually managed to have my baby before I turned 39.

MARGARET And how old is your baby now?

GLORIA Eight-and-a-half months.

MARGARET What was it about being a mother that attracted you?

GLORIA I don't know that I thought I would like it. I just knew that it would happen. It just felt natural somehow, though it didn't feel so natural when it actually happened.

MARGARET How did it feel when it actually happened?

GLORIA I was quite astounded by the whole experience. First of all, the pregnancy was quite interesting, and mine was fairly easy. I found it a really strange concept to have another human being growing inside me and getting bigger and bigger and rolling over and jumping and kicking. The birth came as a total shock. Although I knew it was going to be devastating, it was more than I bargained for.

MARGARET In what way?

GLORIA It was fast and easy, relatively speaking, but the pain was astonishing. I never dreamed that I could handle anything like that, and I was really quite proud of myself for having done so, although I never really thought anyone understood what it was that I went through, even me.

MARGARET You mean you don't remember?

GLORIA I do remember saying, 'I don't ever want to talk

about this again. As far as I'm concerned, the stork brought her.'

MARGARET Did no one tell you there would be pain, or did you feel it was a big secret surprise?

GLORIA No, people had told me it was unbelievable, that it was impossible to describe, and that I probably wouldn't believe it when it happened and or believe it afterwards. I had also been to four births before—three home births and one hospital birth—which was one of the reasons I had postponed having a baby for so long.

MARGARET But now she's here, and you can just barely remember. Would you do it again?

GLORIA I don't think so. One is enough. One is plenty. One is wonderful. I can't imagine doing it again. I can't imagine having more than one. I think that I would be completely beside myself.

MARGARET Why would it seem so difficult for you?

GLORIA Having two tiny little children just seems like a colossal amount of work to me. I don't see how I could possibly keep up with it. And having got to know this girl so well, I wonder what it would be like to have to deal with somebody else, to have to deal with another baby. It amazes me really. It's quite a complex issue.

MARGARET And yet you had a sister. You were raised in a family of more than one.

GLORIA Yes.

MARGARET Tell me about the rest of your experience. Had you decided before the birth to breast-feed?

GLORIA Yes, it was just an assumption that I would have a baby and everything would be fine, and she would be breast-fed for a year, probably, and get into solid foods at about six months. It was a sort of prior knowledge.

MARGARET Where did the idea come from that you would do it that way?

GLORIA I guess it was amassed over the years, from friends who had had children and different theories and ideas of life. They all, of course, breast-fed their children for at least two years. I thought that was a bit excessive in this day and age, so I decided not to go quite that far. I had a phobia about childbirth.

It was so strong that I hated even to say the word out loud. I was terrified of the whole notion. My emphasis was so much on labour and birth that I didn't think there would be anything to think about afterwards. You have a baby, and then you breast-feed the baby, and then life goes on—it's wonderful. That's not how it happened.

MARGARET What did happen?

GLORIA Well, first of all she was three weeks early, and I wasn't prepared. I don't know if anybody is ever prepared. My labour lasted all night, and I didn't sleep until quite late the next night. So I got kind of exhausted from the start, and that exhaustion seemed only to get worse. Being woken up to breast-feed in the night was totally exhausting and quite shocking to me. Although I wanted to do it, the actual, physical me having to wake up several times in the night and feed her became quite amazing. Plus, while I was in hospital I started having problems with my nipples. This wasn't supposed to happen, because I have dark hair and dark skin and they said, 'Oh, no, this only happens to blonds with fair skin. I can't believe you are having trouble. Try lanolin.'

There was quite a succession of nurses, and each one had different methods and theories, and everyone agreed that my baby was latching on marvellously, but there was some other kind of mythological problem we could not put our fingers on. Each day I was in more pain and more exhausted, and finally they said, 'Okay, give her some glucose water so you can sleep at night!' I went home in a state of absolute, utter, and complete exhaustion, with a baby who woke up virtually every hour for the first couple of days.

It took two weeks for my nipples to heal and feel less excruciating. Then the baby didn't seem to be plumping up as a baby should, and a Public Health nurse came around to visit. I had been seeing a doctor who said, 'This baby is not really gaining as quickly as she should, and you look exhausted. Why don't you give her some formula so that you can sleep?' I was just horrified at the thought, thinking that formula was absolute poison—having boycotted formula for the Third World countries for years, the thought of it just made me shudder. I said that I would try anything else. I'd get up every half hour if that would help. Finally, after two weeks, the Public Health nurse came to my house and weighed the baby. She hadn't gained an ounce. In fact she had lost weight, as newborns do, and hadn't gained an ounce back. The nurse went into a total panic, absolutely scared the living daylights out of me. I looked at my baby as if she were an emaciated little skeletal thing lying there on the scale. The nurse was saying that I would have to give her Enfalac immediately and feed it to her from a spoon so she wouldn't get nipple confusion, and I musn't feed her from a bottle—and on and on and on—until I was just devastated. My sister and I escorted her out the door.

I was feeling quite emotional from the whole hormone disruption of childbirth and nursing. My sister said, 'It's not just you. That woman was terrible, and she put you in a panic, and there is nothing to panic about.' I had a midwife who was present at my birth as well, and she came around, and she said—how did she put it?—'She's not in any physical distress.' She suggested I might have to supplement, but not to panic. I didn't want this child to suffer just because of my philosophies about what to feed her, so we decided to try the Enfalac, but also to try the breast-feeding clinic at Vancouver General Hospital. I went through the elaborate process of weighing her and then breast-feeding, and then weighing her again to see how many ounces or drops she had taken in. They measure the minutest quantities.

I wound up using every device that has been invented to try and increase my milk supply—herbal teas, an electric breast-pump, and what they call a 'supplementary nursing system,' which is a little tiny bottle you ring around your neck full of formula, with little tiny tubes that come out at the nipple so that the baby is still sucking at the nipple to create more milk. It got to the point where my house was littered with all this debris and paraphernalia, potions and books, and, needless to say, I was not in very good shape. I was exhausted, I was unhappy. I was crying all the time. The baby at this point was growing, because she was getting formula. The first bottled formula was actually given to her by her father, and I just sat in the corner and cried my eyes out. I cried, first of all because I was devastated, and second, because she was obviously starving—she gobbled down the bottle, and I thought, God, I've been starving the baby because of my own selfish theories. There were some pieces of placenta that hadn't been expelled during the birth, and some came out a week later, and the doctor for some reason didn't think I needed an ultrasound. The women at the breast-feeding clinic said that if it wasn't all out, then my breast-milk wouldn't fully come in, because the birth process wasn't over. I wound up going for a D&C. That was quite horrifying and shocking, the fact that I was right all along—that I did have something else happening, no wonder I didn't have enough milk—plus I am going to have to go into the hospital and have a general anaesthetic, and what am I going to do with my milk? So I went and did it.

MARGARET You had a general anaesthetic?

GLORIA Yes, and a D&C. I got an electric breast-pump and pumped my milk for 24 hours. And my sister baby-sat—which was wonderful—and it surprised me how much formula the baby went through when I wasn't actually breast-feeding her. It was an indication that she was getting some breast-milk out of me, which was nice to see. Then we went back to the clinic and they said, 'Now you're going to take off; now we're going to see some action!' I got all excited and waited for when this huge amount of milk would come spurting out. I waited and waited, and another week went by and another, and I kept going to the clinic and they said, 'Well, maybe because the milk didn't start properly it won't start properly at all.'

I was getting more and more disappointed and talking to people at the La Leche League who said, 'Well, my milk didn't really start until the baby was six weeks old.' As the weeks ticked by, I kept thinking, Next week I'm sure I'll have this figured out. In any case, it never did really come in, and many of my friends couldn't imagine not having enough milk. They'd had their kids 17 years ago, when they were all living in the forest, breast-feeding them for years and years, so they couldn't believe there was such a thing as not enough milk. She was probably four months old when I said to myself, 'You have a supplemented baby, so what! She's gorgeous, she's fine, you are breast-feeding, and someone else can also give her a bottle. What are you complaining about?' I started to relax and I looked at all the gadgets and gizmos that had collected in my kitchen and thought, Good grief, get rid of this stuff!

MARGARET Why was it so emotionally devastating for you to think you couldn't breast-feed your baby?

GLORIA It was twofold. The importance of breast-feeding had been hammered into me. I think I was breast-fed for three months, and I don't know if I was supplemented at this time—in fact I didn't get to talk to my mother about it. But I wondered, Why did she stop at three months? Now I know. She probably didn't have enough milk either, and it was the vogue at that point not to, whereas the people I hung around with in the woods and streams and meadows of rural Ontario, Nova Scotia, and British Columbia were reacting to that upbringing and saying none of that was good, and some of the doctors have taken on that philosophy. My doctor recommended not starting on solid foods too early, but it used to be the practice to feed them solids as soon as possible.

I thought breast-milk was the most nutritionally wonderful stuff for my baby and that, in order for her to have all the benefits of a wonderful life, she should be breast-fed and that's that. And nutritionally speaking, I just thought Enfalac was made of so much junk, I couldn't even bring myself to read the label. I felt like a failure as a woman, because I kept waiting for the magical moment when all this milk would come rushing in—the moment when I would finally fulfil my destiny to offer all this nourishment from these huge breasts to this beautiful baby, and life would be complete. It didn't happen this way.

The Cart Before the Horse

First the Kid, Then the Partner

Mary Morris, born in 1947 in Highland Park, Illinois
Mother of Kate
Interviewed by Susan Swan

SUSAN Mary, you have one daughter, Katie. How old is she?

MARY She's four-and-a-half years old. I had her when I was almost 40 years old. I was 39 and three quarters. I was a single parent for a couple of years with her.

SUSAN And you have written a number of books.

MARY I've published six books. Two volumes of short stories, two travel memoirs, and two novels. I basically alternate between fiction and non-fiction in that way.

SUSAN Do you have a preference?

MARY Fiction. I'd much rather be making up stories, but the non-fiction is fairly lucrative for me. So it's part of what I do to pay the bills, since I published *Nothing to Declare: Memoirs of a Woman Traveling Alone*, which is about my travels alone in Latin America. It did quite well, and I've stopped teaching on a regular basis.

SUSAN Can you tell me when you first thought of having a child? How old you were? Where you were?

MARY I think in my mid-thirties. When I was living in Mexico. I was living with very impoverished Mexicans, and they had lots of children, and the children—it was a very bad time in my life—and the children would come over to borrow things. I remember a day when one little girl, Lisa, hurt herself. She was about four or five years old. Her mother was away. She ran to me for comfort. Comforting that child was such a healing thing for me. It was so surprising to me that she'd come to me. I really hadn't paid much attention to children until then, I was one of those people—I never knew what to give people for wedding gifts or baby gifts. I was just like a wonderful short story by Laurie Colwin called 'The Lone Pilgrim,' about being a single woman among families and married people and not knowing how to behave. I remember that child running to my arms, and that made me feel that I wanted a child.

SUSAN You hadn't been able to relate to children much up to this point?

MARY My friends didn't really have children. They all put careers first. Not many of my friends had good relationships with men. I just wasn't exposed to children. I felt—how can I say this?—I think our lives lead us in the directions that we're going, and I think that I had really resisted being around children or married people at a certain period of my life, because I didn't think that would happen to me. I really felt that those joys of family—for whatever reason—and perhaps because I'd chosen a career—weren't going to be available to me. I just hadn't gone in that direction.

SUSAN It was like that old movie, *The Red Shoes*. You had to either choose your work or love?

MARY I used to read the biographies of woman writers. In college, I remember reading these biographies. The women writers that I admired just didn't have children. Very few were married in any traditional way. George Eliot had a relationship for 30 years and so on, but none of them really had what I would call a traditional situation. It seemed to me that, if I wanted to be a serious writer, which is what I wanted to be, it was a sacrifice I'd have to make.

SUSAN Where were you living in Mexico?

MARY A place called San Miguel de Allende.

SUSAN And after this experience with the little girl, what did you do about your insight?

MARY I don't know that I did anything, except that I felt more open to the possibility of children in my life. Of course, it occurred to me that a man was probably an important element in this problem—

SUSAN [*laughs*]

MARY —and that I would have to do something about that, so when I got back from Mexico, I met a man that I had a rather extensive, three-year relationship with, and I really felt that he was my last-ditch effort at being in a normal relationship. I was 32 when I went to Mexico. This man was completely wrong for me. Emotionally, he was completely not the right person. He had a wrist-watch with an alarm that rang when there was something that he needed to do. We would be down in Soho having brunch and shopping for wonderful things, and all of a sudden the alarm would go off, and the football game was going to start, and so—

SUSAN [*laughs*]

MARY He was not the right man for me. But he was Jewish and I'm Jewish—and he was smart. He was a documentary filmmaker, and he worked in TV news, and blah, blah, blah. When that broke up, I was devastated, because I was—by then I was about 36, and I felt my chances of having anything normal were over, I really felt I was going to live my life alone at that point.

SUSAN What happened then?

MARY Then I got very involved with a man who was in the process of separating from his wife, but he had children, teenaged children. He was older than I was, and I was truly madly in love with him, but it was a nightmare. He's very well known in his field. He travels around the world all the time. He was never home. He was never there.

SUSAN Another impossible man.

MARY Yes, it was completely absurd. I truly fell madly in love with him and very much wanted to have a family with him. I wanted to have a child with him, even though he was quite old, although he was very strong and healthy. He had other children, he had had several bad marriages. It was really an absurd situation, but I was crazy about him. Actually, it was Margaret Atwood who encouraged me. I did an interview with her for the *Paris Review*, and I was very interested in the way Margaret combined having a career and having a daughter and the way that's played out in her life. When I interviewed her for the *Paris Review*, I think it was in 1986, I asked her about it. 'Oh, you can do it,' she said, 'For the first couple of years your hormones are screwed up, but you can definitely have a child.' And so, quite bluntly—it was in 1986—a man I'd been involved with for a number of years and I went to China, and I got pregnant. I assumed we'd get married. I just assumed that.

SUSAN So Margaret Atwood gave you courage.

MARY She did. But the thing about Margaret was that she was in a stable relationship when she had Jess, and she was also quite stable in her career and successful at that point. I was getting more stable professionally, but still was not in a secure place—and I was in a very questionable relationship when I got pregnant.

SUSAN Then what happened?

MARY I conceived the child who's now my daughter. I was on a trip around the world, the trip that *Wall to Wall* is about. I was going from Beijing to Berlin by rail, and in the middle of that journey, I realized that I was pregnant. I'd had a very very serious illness in Mexico in 1978, and I didn't think that I could even have a child, so for lots of reasons I really didn't think I was pregnant for quite a while. Then it dawned on me that, yes, in fact, I was. I called my companion—who was in New York *en route* to New Zealand—and here I was in Moscow *en route* to Berlin—and told him that I was going to have a child. He said, 'Well that's great. That's wonderful. We'll talk about it when we get back.' He went off to New Zealand, I went back to New York, and I was supposed to meet him.

I remember it was fourth of July weekend, he was coming back from New Zealand, he called me from Honolulu, and I told him that I was two-and-a-half months pregnant, and I was very excited. There was dead silence on the phone between New York and Honolulu. I realized he was absolutely not interested in any kind of commitment, even though we'd been together for a long time. So I decided to have an abortion.

I was very devastated by the whole situation. I really felt that this was it. I was going to have an abortion, I was going to be 40, and I was going to be alone. I called my parents. I told my mother I was pregnant and that I was going to have an abortion. I told her not to tell my father no matter what. The next thing I know, my father calls and he goes, 'Look, your mother told me everything, you're going to be 40, and men come and go, you may as well have this baby.' The thing was, I had no idea what I was getting myself into. The thought of having a child seemed great. I thought, Okay, I'll have a child. When I told my friends and everybody, I got lots of attention. When I was pregnant, it was the most wonderful thing in the world. I felt great, and I looked beautiful, and I had lots of people there, and my friends were wonderful. Everything was wonderful.

SUSAN You had a network of family and friends.

MARY Yes, it was great. Everybody was supportive. Everybody was there. Then I had this little baby, and I didn't know what to do. I was beside myself.

SUSAN Where were you living then?

MARY I was living in a one-bedroom apartment in New York City that had been my studio, my workspace, my home for about 10 years. Suddenly I had this baby's crib and all this baby's paraphernalia. I had to move my books into storage, and I had to rearrange my office. Ultimately, I had to take an office out of the house. I watched my life being taken over. I was totally unprepared for this.

When I was pregnant, I had a dream. I dreamed that I was sitting with Margaret Atwood under a tree. It was a very beautiful setting, and she was telling me how wonderful motherhood is and how wonderful it feels to hold a child in your arms. I looked on the ground and lying next to me was a dead squirrel. And a butcher knife. I took the butcher knife and, while she was droning on and on about the wonders of motherhood, I started hacking at the squirrel. All of a sudden it inverted itself and became alive. Like a foetus, essentially. It began to move through the garden eating all the small animals—there were little deer and rabbits. It began to devour everything around it. It was a feeling of, on the one hand listening to what Margaret was saying, which was that motherhood was a joyous experience, and on the other hand, seeing this thing devouring everything around it. I think I was really caught between the desire for this person to love and have and share and grow with in my life and the feeling of being devoured and taken over and destroyed.

SUSAN The child as vampire. That cannibalizes its parent.

MARY Right.

SUSAN I suppose as a writer this would involve threatening your work time.

MARY Yes, the whole thing. I had always worked in a very regimented way. I had to get up first thing in the morning, nobody could bother me. Nobody could talk to me. I had to have my coffee. I had to go right to my desk. I couldn't interact. All of a sudden, forget it! I had to deal with a baby-sitter, I had to deal with 10 phone calls from my mother, I had to deal with the baby, for god's sake. My ideal way to get up in the morning is to have a book and a yellow pad and a nice cup of coffee and just sort of hang out in bed for a couple of hours while my thoughts get going. Well, that was blown out the window. I never do that any more. I never thought I could watch an episode of 'Sesame Street,' make somebody's lunch, walk them to school, do the morning errands, arrange for afternoon baby-sitting, and come back and get some work done, but I do.

SUSAN Is that your day in a nutshell?

MARY Yes, my day now. And it's very odd, because I've never been more productive, and I feel incredibly focused. I feel that motherhood has transformed my life only for the better, but it's a completely different structure. There's no such thing as down time, or time to do nothing.

SUSAN Your life has changed again. Now you have a partner.

MARY Yes, I was with Katie alone for two years. Then Larry came into our lives when she was 18 months old, but came in in a permanent way when she was two years old. He has been partner, helper, companion, you name it, whatever a person can be for someone else. It's a totally shared, committed situation. I really don't know how any woman does it, without someone who's in a sharing situation to some extent.

SUSAN Well, there's daycare, speaking as a woman who didn't have a supportive mate—though I did have an ex-husband who put a lot of time and energy into my daughter. But tell me, when you were in Manhattan the first two years on your own, did you get any writing done then?

MARY I got an enormous amount done. I had no choice. I had to support the child. The first year of her life—this was actually quite wonderful, because I was on the final semester of an eight-year contract to Princeton University. I didn't know what I was going to do. I needed the salary. I was afraid they were going to take my salary away. I was going to have the baby in January, so someone suggested to me that I was probably eligible for maternity benefits, which hadn't occurred to me. I called up Benefits and said to them, 'I'm on the final semester of a contract. I won't be teaching at Princeton again, and I need to know, what do I need to do to have maternity benefits?' They said, 'You need to be pregnant.' I said, 'How long can I have my benefits?' And they said, 'For one semester.' So the last semester that I was at Princeton, I got my full salary, which was great.

Then I needed a job. I took a job at the University of California, and that was really the worst year of my life, because I had to pack up the baby, and myself, and leave the person who was then my nanny, or helper. I really believe in angels, and I really believe that she was an angel who was sent to me, because she was just so wonderful—helped in ways that I never would have thought possible. It was really like a guardian angel had come and taken care of me and then flew away.

SUSAN How did she help you?

MARY Katie was about three weeks old. My mother had been with me—my mother and I had slept in the same bed for about two weeks. I love my mother very much, but sleeping with her in the same bed, it's just not something I would do very comfortably. But we did it. We took care of the baby around the clock. Then my mother had to go back. She said, 'Look, you need help, you can't be alone with the baby.' I had a housekeeper who came in about five hours a day. My mom said, 'Get someone to come in at night for the first couple of weeks or so, just so you're not alone.' I didn't even know what to do with the baby. And there was no mate there. I didn't have a spouse. I was alone. I didn't know what to do with this, this thing.

SUSAN Were you breast-feeding?

MARY Yes, I was breast-feeding. Kate was very demanding about breast-feeding. Also, it was terrible because, three weeks after she was born, *The New York Times* assigned me the 'Hers' column. I had to do these 'Hers' columns while I had this little baby. They would call me at 10 o'clock at night—which was often her feeding time—and say they had to do an edit for the next day. And so I put the baby on my breast with a pillow and sat at the word processor with the phone tucked in my ear, and edited, and twice I dropped the phone on her head—I'm surprised she's not brain-damaged—but I had no choice. They'd call me, I'd say, 'I've got a little baby, what can I do?' And they'd say, 'We're sorry, but we're going to press, we've got to go over these changes with you.'

After a few weeks of this, I called an agency, and they sent me a very odd woman. She talked very strangely. She was from Jamaica. She looked peculiar. Her hair was green, her hair was turning green—which she apologized for. She had no eyebrows, but what she had was painted on blue. She would come in and take off her clothes and put on a nurse's outfit and sit in a chair next to me and watch me go to sleep, if you can imagine this. I would say to her, 'Could you go somewhere?' I had to tell her to go into another room. The first night she was there, I was very uncomfortable. She left, and she came back. The next night, when I woke up in the morning, I realized that all the baby's clothes had been hand-washed and hung up. She'd given the baby a bottle at the right time so that I had a few hours to myself before the baby got up. It was like Tinkerbell. I felt that a little magic spirit had come in and taken over.

SUSAN She knew what to do.

MARY She knew exactly what to do. I was sleeping. She just took care of everything. Then one morning, I woke up and heard her say to somebody—I didn't know at the time it was to Katie, to the baby—I heard her say, 'It's snowing outside. You better cancel all your appointments today.' I went downstairs and she was holding Katie up to the window and showing her the snow, and I thought, This woman has been sent to help me. I said to her, 'Inez, I don't know how long I can afford you, but would you consider working nights for me and helping me out during the day?' And she did for a long time. For a long time she worked nights, until two or three in the afternoon. She'd go home for a couple of hours to the Bronx and come back at 10 o'clock at night. So I could have sleep. She just took care of me. She was very expensive, but I just needed help. I had to earn a living. I had to work. Psychologically, I needed help.

SUSAN How expensive? May I ask?

MARY Yes, my parents helped me out. For several months I paid her $400 a week, but she worked maybe 16 hours a day.

SUSAN You don't have to convince me. I'm sure she earned every penny of it.

MARY She earned every penny of it. For those few months, my parents gave me the money. They said, when I said I would have the baby, they said, 'We'll help you as much as we can.' I think the only way a person can have a baby on their own is if they're independent financially, or if they have someone who can help them out. I don't know how women without resources —poor women—do it.

SUSAN Did your sense of yourself change, begin to change, during this period?

MARY Once I had a baby, I got very depressed. It really hadn't occurred to me that my life was irrevocably, utterly changed. Before I had a baby, I had travelled anywhere I wanted, whenever I wanted. I went to a restaurant whenever I wanted. Suddenly, I can't go to the corner. I can't buy a quart of orange juice without arranging something. I had to call a friend upstairs. I'd sit there and think to myself, What could happen if I ran to the corner for toilet paper? Obviously this doesn't happen so much to women who have a mate. Someone can be home while you go out.

SUSAN I'm a single mother. I remember the problem very well. I lived in a co-op, but just the logistics of doing simple chores suddenly became very problematic.

MARY Yes, I had delivery people coming to my house all the time—everything was brought in. To their credit, friends would call and say, 'I'm going to the store, can I get you anything?' It was winter, and that wasn't the easiest time to be a single parent alone with a newborn baby. Also, I felt very rejected by her father, who was still in the picture but was absolutely no help. At all.

SUSAN So you were depressed. What form did this depression take? Were you just generally blue, or did you feel hysterical at times?

MARY I think, to my credit, I really accepted the responsibility of my daughter, and I've never taken things out on her. If I've been upset about something, I've always said to her, 'Mommy's upset because I have to work too hard, we don't have money right now.' I've always tried to explain to her. She's always helped me, she's always been there for me. That actually is not my basic personality trait. My basic personality trait is to make the people around me suffer.

SUSAN [*laughs*] You want people to be depressed or upset with you.

MARY Or to spend a lot of time getting me back to where I want to be. If things are bothering me, poor Larry has to spend an awful lot of his free time talking to me about me or trying to get me back on a track. Before I had Katie, I must admit, I had an irrational temper. A family trait.

SUSAN What sort of things would you do?

MARY I'd just blow up.

SUSAN Not wrap golf clubs around a tree, or—

MARY No, it wasn't violent. Well, occasionally it was violent, but if it was violent it was sort of, I don't know, stupid, throwing dishes, the stupid kind of violent things. Occasionally, Katie's biological father really drove me insane. He was really crazy, and he really made me crazy.

SUSAN Were you still seeing him then, during this two-year period you were in Manhattan?

MARY I was seeing him, and I was very involved with him in a complicated psychological way, but there was something about having a child that made me want to be healthy. It made me not want to lose my temper. It made me not want to take things out on somebody else. And it made me want to get out of a sick relationship. I could let him disappoint me, I could let him abandon me, I could let him call me up and say, 'I love you so much that you just can't believe it, but I just can't be there for you for the next few months.' You know?

SUSAN [*laughs*]

MARY 'I'm just unavailable. I have to be in The Hague, and then I have to be—,' wherever. He would do things like call me from India. He'd say, 'Hi, I can't talk, but I just wanted to call.' I'd say, 'What are you calling me from India for if you can't talk?' The kinds of things that make you crazy. I would have put up with that, probably for the rest of my life, because my self-esteem wasn't so great in terms of men. This man was a very charismatic, famous, glamorous man. So why not put up with it? But I didn't want my daughter to be disappointed. I didn't want her to be hurt in that way. I didn't want her to be getting calls from India from a father she loved who didn't have time to talk. I took the job in California, and I slowly separated myself from him.

SUSAN What is his situation *vis à vis* your daughter? Does he exercise any parental rights? Or duties?

MARY He gave those up. I gave him a choice, a legal choice. I said to him, 'If you want to be involved with her, you sign an affidavit accepting paternity, you agree to support and visitation, and we have a legal agreement about her. Or, you sign this piece of paper and you give it all up.' For her. For me—I don't care. If she wants to see him, I don't care. But my feeling was, he is the kind of person who will flit in and out of people's lives as he sees fit. I didn't want this child disappointed in the way that I'd been disappointed. I didn't want her to feel abandoned, and she doesn't. I said to him, 'This is what you can do. You can accept responsibility or you can give up paternal rights.' He gave up his paternal rights. Larry has adopted her now.

SUSAN So you went to California to do this teaching job. When she was a year old? And this was the worst year of your life?

MARY She wasn't a year old, she was eight months old. I had no friends. I was living in the most beautiful place on the continental United States. I was living right on the Pacific Ocean. I had nobody to be with. Nobody to help me. I hired a very sweet Mexican woman whom I had nothing in common with. Inez and I were really a match. We were really friends. This other woman, it was like having a servant or something. I felt very uncomfortable with her. She was not very with it. She had a lot of trouble taking care of things. I was not in good shape. I had to do a job that I didn't really want to be doing.

SUSAN This was the teaching job. How many courses?

MARY Three courses a quarter.

SUSAN Ooh.

MARY And I had to direct the undergraduate writing program. I had a lot of work, and I didn't have a lot of money. On the weekend—my careperson would leave on Friday night and come back on Monday morning—I was alone with a little baby and a lot of work to do. From Friday night until Monday morning.

SUSAN How did you do your work?

MARY I don't think I worked much on the weekends. I tried to put Katie down to sleep, but Katie has never napped. She's never been a sleeper. I'd try to get her to go to bed at eight o'clock at night, and everybody told me what to do, and I did what the book said, and it didn't matter. She'd scream her head off until 10:30 at night. She'd never go to sleep at eight o'clock. I just did what I could. I had friends in L.A., so I'd put the baby in the car and go to L.A. for the weekends as best I could. I finally got a few friends where I was living. One of my best friends moved there, but she was also having problems. We were all having problems. It was awful. It was really awful. I'll give you a perfect example. My second Mother's Day, Katie was 16 months old. This was actually great. I'd just published *Nothing to Declare*. I had got a message at school that a journalist, a reporter from *The Daily Planet*—which is Superman's newspaper, Clark Kent works for *The Daily Planet*—wanted to interview me. I mean, I was living in this weird place in California, I said, 'Okay, so if a reporter from *The Daily Planet* wants to interview me, so what?' It turned out she was a reporter for *The Daily Pilot*.

SUSAN [*laughs*]

MARY And a very nice reporter she was. We had a lovely interview. We said good-bye. The Sunday morning of Mother's Day, I was alone in Southern California. I had plans in the later afternoon, but basically I was alone. Katie got up at six o'clock in the morning. I fed her, I gave her a bath, I got her dressed, I made her breakfast. I didn't put her tray in properly, she pushed the tray and all the food fell out, she fell out of her high chair, I had on these filthy dirty sweat-pants, and I couldn't take a shower because she'd scream when I took a shower because she couldn't see me. It was about 8:30 in the morning, and I was really going to have a breakdown. I was going to lose it. I actually called a friend and I said, 'I really don't think I can take it, I just don't know what to do.' Then I looked up and coming up my garden path was the reporter from *The Daily Pilot* in a workout suit, Spandex, with an enormous bouquet of flowers. She came and she knocked on my door and she said, 'I know it's Mother's Day and you're alone, so I brought you flowers.' I burst out crying. I burst out crying in this woman's arms. I was beside myself. I really was beside myself.

SUSAN That's a wonderful story. I think that's every mother's fantasy when they're alone, and in a desperate situation, to have somebody step out of the blue and acknowledge what you're going through.

MARY Yes. The fact is, you can't talk to a little baby. It only cares to have its needs met. This stuff about falling in love with your child and all that—I mean, I loved my daughter, but I think if I'd had a real mate with me and we'd had a sharing situation, it would've been a completely different ball game, but you know, being alone with her, I think I really experienced motherhood at its most—

SUSAN Harrowing?

MARY Well, excruciating. Maybe for women who don't have ambitions for themselves, it's different. There were things I wanted to do. I used to work seven days a week. I'd work whenever I felt like it, I'd read whenever I felt like it, and all of a sudden—it was terrible.

SUSAN Feeling frustrated about your work time being taken over, was this your biggest problem after you'd got used to the fact that you had a child in your life? Let's talk about your problems.

MARY I started thinking of prisoners and invalids and mothers in the same breath. I felt the confinement, the simple task of getting out the door. It's funny, because there's a prison near where we live here, and I look at those prisoners—I can see them, I can see their shadows. I feel that I can understand better what they've been through because I've been a single mother, because I've been in a situation where you can't go to a movie, you can't do the things that you normally do to take care of yourself, to feel better. You can't do them. Just the task of going to a friend's and hanging out. Everything becomes an effort. I used to go anywhere whenever I wanted. That was really hard for me.

SUSAN When did Larry come into your life, and how did you meet him?

MARY My second angel, Larry, came in when Katie was 18 months old, and I had really closed the door on Katie's father. I had asked him for some money—$200 a month—to help me with childcare and he said no. Then he bought a new car, an expensive dog, for his teenage son. It became clear to me that he was seeing other women. I started to put it all together and told him never to contact me again. It wasn't even so much for me. It was for the baby. I didn't want this man traipsing through her life the way I had allowed him to traipse through mine.

SUSAN I understand what you're talking about very well, because it seemed that with the birth of my daughter, I gained powers of self-assertion that I hadn't claimed before. To have a child somehow gave me the right to have my own rights. It's sad in a way that we would need a child to do that for us, but I guess it's wonderful that they can provide that.

MARY I feel that I've always wanted to be empowered, and if this is the way that I became empowered, fine. I think there's probably lots of women who aren't so lucky, who just continue going on dragging through the life that they've lived. I knew that this was wrong, and I didn't have the willpower to stop it. But I really couldn't bear to see her hurt in the ways that I had been hurt.

SUSAN No, that makes perfect sense to me. Now, your second angel—he has legally adopted your daughter.

MARY We're one court date away from legal adoption.

SUSAN How did your life change when he came into it and became a full-time partner and father figure for your child?

MARY I don't know if I should even talk about this. Because I've talked to so many women, I think my experience with Larry is so unique. He is really a male whose ego, it's very hard to explain what his ego's like, but he's the most grounded, centred—a tai-chi-type person. When I met him, I was at a rock-bottom point. I had been separated, broken up with Katie's father for several months, and I was really in pain over it. I was teaching at a conference in Virginia. As my mother says, 'When a Canadian drives down from North Bay, Canada in an un-airconditioned car to Richmond, Virginia in a July heat wave, it's fate.' [*laughter*]

It was really hot. He'd come to the conference. He was the only person from another country or another place besides Virginia that was at the conference. I was the teacher. He was supposed to be in another class—the woman who ran the conference, who has since become a very good friend of ours, took a look at him and thought he'd be happier in my class, so he became my student. The first time Larry saw Katie was when my mother and Katie and my nephew arrived at the airport in Richmond—I had a week alone at the conference, and then my mother came. Katie went running off the airplane and just dashed down the platform, and she was gone in the crowd of people at the airport. I didn't know what to do, and I said, 'Larry, go get her!' He just dashed after her and went and got her, halfway down the terminal. It's been like that ever since. He's never batted an eye. He's never said to me, 'You get up, it's your daughter.' He's always said things like, 'If you want to work, I'll take care of her. I'll take her out while you do what you need to do.' There's never been a moment when this man hasn't expressed anything but complete acceptance of this role. He's really a feminized male, a feminist male, but he's still a man.

SUSAN Did your life change dramatically then, do you find it easier to be a mother with a full-time mate?

MARY Oh, my life changed dramatically. I really think—I don't want to get too religious here—I mean, I am a fairly religious person in a way—

SUSAN [*laughs*] Oh, you can get religious.

MARY —but I really feel that I was at a point where I had been tested as far as I could go. Somebody knew that I was at a point where I needed help. I really feel it was a gift. And my life, yes, my relationship with my daughter changed.

SUSAN Can you tell me how?

MARY I enjoyed being with her more, because I didn't have to be with her every moment that I wasn't paying someone to take care of her.

SUSAN Your story is really one of experiencing two faces of motherhood. You've experienced what it's like to be a single mother, and now you're experiencing what's it like to be in a more traditional family—although from what you've said, your mate is not a traditional father. Would you tell me how your life has changed with Larry?

MARY I'm just a much better mother. Before I was either working or taking care of Kate. There was no such thing as being able to go for a walk in the park or visit a friend, or go and do something, without paying someone to look after Kate. Now Larry and I share. I cook, Larry cleans up. I do all the night-time stuff. Getting her down to sleep, reading to her, I sing songs and all that. He does all the morning stuff. He makes breakfast, he makes her lunch, he gets her dressed in the morning. We split things that way. We work it out. One of us will take her to school and one of us will pick her up. I'll make dinner, and we'll eat about seven. Then she'll get her bath at about 7:30. At 8:00 she can watch a short movie, or preferably, we'll play with her. We don't let her watch more than a couple of movies a week. It depends on how tired she is, and it depends on what demands are on us. Then usually, from about 8:00 until 10:00, I will read to her, play with her, sing, whatever we do until she's ready for bed. This is one of the things I notice about being a woman with a career. It's very hard for me to put her to sleep at eight o'clock at night. Friends I know who were full-time mothers said that they were with their kids all day long, so by seven o'clock at night they were ready to get them ready for bed. Whereas I haven't seen her all day, so I want to have that little bit of time with her. That's important to me.

The problem is, I'm exhausted by the time I get her to bed. I don't want to talk. I just read, and I usually fall asleep reading. It's not great for the marriage. Larry said, and I think rightly so, that I've kind of clung to her babyhood, and I've felt—perhaps because I was a single parent, and I had to work very hard to earn a living for us—that there were moments I missed. So I try to kind of get them back a little bit, and enjoy them a little more—but as a result, I'm not so good at disciplining her on what time she goes to bed.

SUSAN Let's talk about discipline. Do you have a system?

MARY We have a discipline system that's just simply, it's just—the problem is it doesn't work, but we try the best we can. We simply use time out. First of all, Katie is required to help with dinner, she has to help clean up, she has to help with her room. We're trying to teach her, that if she is going to play and have fun—that we're all working very hard to make everything work, that with two parents and two careers where neither career is completely stable, we all have to pitch in. She's got a sense of chores and that sort of thing. There are certain things we won't tolerate. We won't tolerate lying, talking back, or just spoiled behaviour—then she has to be in time out and reflect upon her behaviour. The problem is, she just won't do it. We tell her she has to go to her room, and she just won't do it—and gets in a terrible state about it. So—

SUSAN So time out doesn't really work.

MARY Well, what we basically do is, Larry picks her up and dumps her in her room and makes her sit there. But she won't go on her own.

SUSAN Does this bring up issues of how you were both disciplined as children?

MARY I think so, because my big issue is losing my temper. My father always lost his temper, and always lost it really irrationally—you'd never know about what or when. I have found that PMS is my best alibi. There are just certain times of the month where, if I'm going to blow, I'm going to blow. I feel that I've got a handle on it, although we have our household stresses and there are times that we've definitely lost it with each other.

SUSAN What would those times be around? Mealtimes, or—

MARY If we're going to have a family argument, Larry and I will argue in the morning, because he will get mad at the way the chores are going ahead. I kind of dawdle and play with her, and he wants things to happen *bang, bang, bang*. We've had our arguments over that. Again, it's my problem of letting go, and I know that, but when Katie was a little baby, after the year in California, I was dropping her off in a daycare centre and—I had to go to work in Washington, actually, and I had to leave her for two days and trust friends to pick her up from the daycare centre—and it was just awful.

SUSAN Have you felt a lot of guilt over her? Because of your work?

MARY It's funny, I have, but she's really well-adjusted, and I can tell that. I feel I have to take credit for some of it, because I've really tried to explain to her what I needed to do, why I needed to work. I've explained to her that it's not only something for money, but it's something that I love to do, or I'm not happy. We have this concept at home of being each other's friend. I'll say to her, 'You know, if you really want to be my friend, let me work for an hour, and I'll play with you.' She really understands that. Also, I'll let her work, I'll give her a stapler and scissors and some envelopes and tell her that this mail has to go out, you know. She'll do her tasks.

SUSAN And you paint with her a lot.

MARY Yes, I paint to relax. It is a slight interest of mine, but unfortunately I'm not very good at it. I would like to be good at it, but I don't know if I'm good at it or not—I just do it. One of the reasons I paint is because I don't care about it, it frees me up in a certain way. Katie and I do a lot of collaborative painting. Today, she was painting, and I got a phone call, and when I came back she had painted a really beautiful painting. Very abstract, colours very beautifully composed, it was beautiful, and she had dabbed balls of colour on it, sort of strategically. I told her this was beautiful—and then she took a paintbrush and she proceeded to mix all these balls together and ruined the painting. I got very upset, and I said, 'Oh, it's beautiful the way it is honey, you should leave it, it's really beautiful.' She said, 'I can paint the way I want to paint, it's my picture. If I want to do it this way, you can't tell me how to do it.'

Of course she was right. On the other hand, she was ruining something that I thought was very beautiful. I really felt a tug within me, between my desire to let my child express herself, on the one hand, and on the other hand, the desire to hold on to this beautiful thing, to have something I could put on the wall, something I could write the date on and stick up. I was very torn, and I really didn't like myself for intruding in her process.

SUSAN How did you resolve it?

MARY We haven't resolved it. I'm going to talk to her later and apologize for having interfered. I think what I should've said to her is, 'I think it's really beautiful the way it is, but it's your picture and you can do what you want with it.'

SUSAN [*laughs*]

MARY I think one of the things I got from my mother as a girl—I came from a fairly controlling family—and I think maybe, because I'd like to paint better, when I see Katie painting a certain way, I'd like to control the situation a little bit, or I feel myself controlling her, and I know it's not good. The next time we paint, if she wants to paint everything black, I think it's her right to paint her picture black.

SUSAN How were you disciplined? You, as a child.

MARY Oh, in a way that probably most people who rear children would think is not very good. Not physically, but psychologically. Things didn't really get talked out very well. I try to teach Katie that if she tells me the truth about something that happened, I might be upset with her, but I won't punish her if she tells me the truth—unless she does something really vicious or something—and she really tells the truth. When she painted on the chair, she told me that she painted on the chair. When she hammered a hole in the floor, she told me. I just remember being screamed at for those things, that a child really doesn't know—if you give a child a hammer and a nail, they'll probably nail it into the wooden floor. They might not know.

SUSAN That's right. Why not? It sounds like there's trust and respect between you and your daughter.

MARY Yes, I think so. I've always respected her from the moment she was born. I felt if she was going to put up with me through these couple of years—and she didn't know what she was getting herself into—I just figured I should really respect her because, to her credit, she's a strong, happy person. She has a great sense of play. She has a great sense of humour. She's basically a very good kid.

SUSAN Okay, I have two last questions. The first one is money. Is that a problem or an issue?

MARY Money is a big problem. It's a problem because neither Larry nor I have permanent jobs. Last year I made an enormous amount of money, which the IRS took an enormous chunk out of. This year, I've made hardly any money. We're living on what I made last year. It's very up and down. We'd very much like to have another child, but there's not that financial stability and, you know, I'm 44, and to have a child without that stability—and there's things I'd like to give Katie. She likes to garden, she likes animals. I'd love to give her a house in the country. On the other hand, I was thinking how my parents gave me everything I wanted except the things I really wanted, and I think she has more of the things she really wants. She has attention, she likes to spend time with us, we like to spend time with her. But yes, money is definitely a problem.

SUSAN Now, the last question. Has being a mother changed your views at all on feminism, women's position in society? Has it effected you in any broader political sense? Or has it just confirmed opinions you already had?

MARY If I could go from the personal to the more political, I think having a child has made me very in touch with poverty, deprivation, injuries to children, both mental and physical. My book *Wall to Wall* ends with me knowing I'm going to have a child, and standing in front of a memorial to an 18-year-old boy who was shot trying to get into West Berlin and realizing that this boy was somebody's child. Before, when a couple of Black kids would be shot in a playground, I'd think, That's not my neighbourhood, I don't live there, I'm safe, I'm here. Now I think, They have mothers, they have families. This is not just somebody else's problem in another part of town. It's made me more aware of the world in a very deep way. The whole notion of cross-fire. I'm obsessed with cross-fire, not because I think something will happen to my child, because I don't live in a neighbourhood—

SUSAN Cross-fire? Can you explain that to me?

MARY Cross-fire is when two gangs are fighting in New York or Los Angeles and they shoot up a block and children are killed. Children are killed every year in New York by stray bullets. A kid walks out of a grocery store at night, and somebody is shooting at a gang member, and the child is killed. It happens all the time. Those stories which I used to read as somebody else's problem, I think of it now as, What if it were my child? Then I think, It's somebody else's child—and it's made me much more aware of a whole political reality. In terms of feminism, I'm certainly more aware of the problems that women have, and it's not just marginal, soft problems. I mean money, child care, equal pay, maternity leave, paternity leave—all the things women fight for. And men have fought for also. They're not just the soft issues of our society. They're the fabric of how the family is structured. It's made my feminism not just the 'see I'm mad at men who aren't nice to me and I'm going to be tough' brand. It's made it a much bigger issue for me.

SUSAN Is there support for single mothers in the United States? Is there any kind of daycare subsidy you can get? Is there much of a network or help? You had your family and friends …

MARY Well it's not like Canada. Canada's medical care, it's safety nets that provide for its citizens—it's really fabulous. When you live in a society where the Supreme Court has ruled that doctors in federal family planning clinics can't tell indigent women about abortion— No. There's not support for single parents. There are state-run daycare centres, and they're horrible. They might not be horrible, I shouldn't say they're horrible, but between the public schools and the daycare centres and health care in this country, there is not real support for somebody who is on their own. I had my own earning power, and I had help from my family. There are lots of people out there who don't have either of those things. It was a privileged situation that I was in. I could've done it on my own with my salary. I would've had to cut back on a lot of things, but I could've done it. But I don't really know how.

SUSAN Is there anything else you want to say about mothering that I haven't asked you?

MARY One of the things I've learned about mothering is that the myth and the reality are so different from one another. Yes, you love your child and all that, but it's not like your average soap commercial. It is really work in the toughest sense of the word—and the next shift's not going to come on. It doesn't go away. I think that most women don't have real preparation for the demands. The rewards we talk about, but the demands—I was not prepared for them.

SUSAN Do you think women are kept deliberately ignorant?

MARY Yes, I would say probably so. I remember going through childbirth thinking to myself, This is horrible, this hurts like hell. Then when I had to breast-feed, breast-feeding was so painful I screamed every time I started to breast-feed, and I said to the nurse, 'Why isn't this in any of the books?' and she laughed and she said, 'Who would breast-feed then, dear, if everyone knew that?' For the first three weeks it hurt like hell. It's not in the books particularly. I think that there is a kind of deliberate romanticization of it. And of marriage too. But more so of child-rearing.

SUSAN Is there a demon in child-raising? A demon of motherhood? What would that be if there is?

MARY I think that motherhood can be a real trap. I know a lot of women, where you're stuck, you can't go anywhere, you're in a marriage that's not going to let you go anywhere. I don't think it's for nothing that most of the great writers who have lived in the last hundred years have been men. The women were too busy taking care of things.

The Floating World
of a Nuclear Mom

Sasha Dupré, born in 1954 in New Westminster, B.C.
Mother of Maréva and Aisha
Interviewed by Margaret Dragu

MARGARET This boat here is called *Sasha*. That's named after you, obviously.

SASHA Actually that was my husband's first gesture when we got together. That was the very first boat I met him around. It used to be one of those fishing boats from Steveston that we converted to a live-aboard. We were sort of dating. The first thing he had me do was scrub the bottom off in pouring rain, and he thought, Whoa! What a woman, she hasn't complained yet! So—

MARGARET I love you, scrape my barnacles. [*laughter*] That's great, when was this?

SASHA Oh, about 1974. That one there was our first real wooden sail-boat—it had been everywhere in the world, but we hadn't. One of those situations, one of those heavy mortgages and trying to get the boat going, and as you're paying off the boat, you also realize the boat is disintegrating faster than you can pay it off.

MARGARET And you hadn't gone anywhere.

SASHA Hadn't gone anywhere. Then we thought, let's get smart, and that's when we started moving on to steel boats.

MARGARET This was the steel cutter, *Alder*? '79 - '81?

SASHA Yes, that's the first metal boat that we built from the beginning and finished. Cut the tree down for the mast up in Jervis Inlet.

MARGARET You built the whole thing?

SASHA The whole thing, and sailed it.

MARGARET Was Maréva around then?

SASHA Maréva was the gleam in her father's eye, and that's the reason we came back—I was pregnant. [*indicates *another boat*] That's the *Maréva*, that bigger boat there, red and green. That yellow one down there is another boat we built while we were building ours.

MARGARET So your better half was working as a ship's carpenter and shipbuilder while you were making your own boats.

SASHA Hm-mm. We built that large one because we were having a family.

MARGARET For the three of you. And where did you travel on that one?

SASHA Down the coast to Mexico and over to Hawaii. We were going to keep going, but then I got pregnant with Aisha. [*laughter*]

MARGARET Another gleam!

SASHA In fact, between *Alder* and *Maréva*, there was probably about five years, because when we were building that, I went back to university and did my practicum so I could get my teaching certificate. That was kind of interesting.

MARGARET You got some education. That was very clever.

SASHA [*laughs*] Trying to find one of those daycares that would take an infant, I think she was 16 months old, while we were finishing the boat off, and saving money, and going to school, and trying to get it ready to go.

MARGARET So, he was working on the boat and you were working on the boat and going to school, and Maréva was in daycare.

SASHA Paul was also working on the side with his father, operating heavy equipment and using his steel-working skills to fix machinery.

MARGARET It must have been hard going to school full-time as well as building—were you living on a boat at the same time?

SASHA Yes, living on the one we were building. [*laughs*]

MARGARET Did you go to Simon Fraser University?

SASHA Yes, because we had the boat in Port Moody. But it meant a lot of driving around. It's really hard because you go through the debate of, I've got my little one, and you take her to the daycare, and you know she loves it, but she stands in the window and cries and waves good-bye and you go, Am I doing the right thing? But it worked out. She was an only child at that time, too, and we thought it would be nice for her to be around other kids, especially when we'd got all these other projects.

MARGARET She had lots of one-on-one time with you when you were sailing.

SASHA Oh, yes.

MARGARET But it must have been hard. You must have felt a bit guilty and—

SASHA Well, you go through that, but you have to think of the greater good. We always talk about quality time, but I think for her it was nice to be around kids her age, because we usually had a lot of adults around at the time. Not a lot of our friends have kids. Or, if they do, they're teenagers, or the parents are going through divorce situations. That's why I liked it with a steady group of teaching staff at the daycare, Rocky Point.

MARGARET Was that part of Simon Fraser?

SASHA No, it was separate. At that time I didn't realize that they had a daycare at Simon Fraser but—

MARGARET This one worked out.

SASHA I think it was better having Maréva somewhere separate from the university, because then, when I was at university, I could totally focus on that. If I knew she was 20 feet away in another room, and I was trying to do research or something, probably, in one of those moments where I felt totally overwhelmed, I'd have thought, Well, I'll just put the books aside. I'll go and see how my daughter is doing, and then I'll come back to it. That would've stretched things out too long. It was better knowing she was taken care of and away, and I could fully concentrate on what I was doing.

MARGARET What is this one, the junk ship?

SASHA Yes. We rigged it—that's the picture with the sails up—so it's called a junk-rigged schooner.

MARGARET It's based on a Chinese system?

SASHA Right, so you don't have to get any extra sails for light airs or for heavy weather. All you do is use the sails like venetian blinds. Raise them or lower them depending on how much you want, and you're not having to run out and do a lot of adjustments or major changes.

MARGARET So you went to Mexico and Hawaii with Maréva and you were pregnant again.

SASHA We were thinking about going on to Australia, because you can have, I mean, people have babies everywhere. Maréva was the first grandchild on both sides, and then we thought, Well, Canada is still a hop, skip, and a jump away, and we've got a good medical system, and all the grandparents are there—I might as well go back home one more time. [*laughs*] Two is the maximum number we're going to have for our family, because if anything happens to us, we could manage. They're company for each other and, at our age, I don't feel I have the energy for more children, and my husband's happy having the two that we have. Also on the boat—

MARGARET You'd have to have a bigger boat!

SASHA No, [*laughs*] it's just so one eye can keep an eye on one person, and the other adult is responsible for the other.

MARGARET It's easier.

SASHA Yes, and for breaking up to do things. There's two of you going off, instead of the odd man out with the third person.

MARGARET So this orange one?

SASHA That's the *Maréva* when we brought it back to Canada again. We were getting ready to sell it.

MARGARET This is the one you all went out on as a foursome?

SASHA That one there.

MARGARET The *Able.*

SASHA *Able.* Because we were able to get out there and do it. Just to leave everything.

MARGARET Great name! So there you were, how old was Aisha?

SASHA She was still in diapers. I remember she toilet-trained herself as a present on Mother's Day. I think she was two then.

MARGARET What a girl!

SASHA We were faced with having to buy paper diapers in France, which were about 40 dollars for 20. We were thinking about building another boat, because we'd sold *Maréva*. Because we're used to doing interiors, we just re-vamped a highway bus and lived on that in the meantime. We were trying to design a new and improved steel boat. Then Paul said, 'Why don't we go to Europe and take a look? There are a lot of innovative designs over there.' One of those great ouzo nights. [*snaps fingers*] We said 'France!' So he flew over first—and found a boat a couple of weeks after doing a mega-tour of Spain and Italy and France, Holland and Germany. I guess he was away about a month altogether.

MARGARET And you were in the meantime living on a bus with the two kids.

SASHA Going, Geez, I wonder what we're going to do next? He found a boat. We sold everything off, flew to Holland, and took the train down to southern France where our boat was. They hauled it out of the water that afternoon. We had jet lag, and I'm going, This is it? It was supposed to be situated in a vineyard, but it was next to a highway, adjacent to the vineyard —we thought, This is going to be interesting. We all just moved on board and started ripping everything out. In France there were few big blue cans in which to put garbage, so we tried a trick we'd heard about in New York. We took our suitcases and the rest of the peeled-off wallpaper out of the boat, and whatever junk we didn't want, plus about a good week's worth of used diapers, packed them all inside, locked them and put them on the road underneath our boat—and about three hours later when it got dark, we heard *urch!! thumpa! thumpa! thumpa!* Someone took our suitcases away! [*laughs*] Full of garbage!

MARGARET They'd have a surprise when they opened them up and found those poopy diapers.

SASHA It was a good joke, yes. They never came back! [*laughter*]

MARGARET You really get involved in a whole community when you're on a big project like that. You've got to find nuts, you've got to find bolts, and you've got to dump garbage.

SASHA Within walking distance. Plus have the kids.

MARGARET And find a place to wash your clothes and hang them up.

SASHA Discreetly. Discreetly.

MARGARET And find out what all the funny rules are everywhere you go. For example, in Etobicoke you can get a fine for hanging your laundry up on Sunday.

SASHA Oh, I believe it.

MARGARET There are strange customs like that all over, that you wouldn't know that you're breaking. Do you speak French? Your husband speaks French?

SASHA Paul is fluent, and I'm learning. I find it so frustrating when there's a bunch of people all talking French, like when we were in Tahiti, and you can hear the energy in their voices and you're going, Uh, what's that? Could you *répetez s'il vous plait?*

MARGARET Also, when you're with someone who's fluent, you do tend to lean on them a bit. Well, you're very social and outgoing, I can see how you would travel well, but it must take extra skill to travel with kids. I find it difficult taking my daughter to Vancouver—to walk or bicycle up to the end of the road and lock the bicycle and get on the bus and go for an hour into town and come back—that seems like a really big deal.

SASHA That's the whole day.

MARGARET That's the whole day.

SASHA [*laughs*] I know!

MARGARET Yet you had two kids, one younger than two, that you whipped on a plane and took off to Holland and then ran around the world in a small boat.

SASHA That might sink! [*laughs*]

MARGARET Perhaps not.

SASHA No, we hit something, Christmas before last, crossing the Atlantic, near Grenada in the West Indies. We were about 600 miles offshore. It was Christmas morning, gorgeous out, one of those perfectly clear, trade mornings. Paul was at the wheel. It was seven in the morning, and I had just lifted some boards to get at the bottled water, when we slammed something. Just [*slaps hands together*] *thwunk!* And the boat stopped and the nose went down. The wind fell out of the sails. We'd been scooting along, six knots, like 40 miles an hour in a car, to be stopped dead, like *whoa!* One of the fellows felt a *twunk!* in his chest because of the ramming, that pressure. And we heard a dull thud, and we're in a steel boat, and if metal hits metal, you hear a clang—in case there was, say, a submerged container that had fallen off ship—but to hear a thud, you think of something organic, so everybody came running up on deck. We kind of skidded, then *whhht!* we were back off again. Everybody looked around for—

MARGARET Rocks?

SASHA No, we checked the chart. We were still out in deep sea, nothing there, no coral reefs or anything. Even if there were, you'd hear a grinding, but we heard a thud which resonated through the hull. And we're a heavy boat. Paul worked out the physics of it, boat speed plus our weight, stopped dead, the mass of the thing that would have to stop us. We didn't see any blood—no leaves or wood. Maybe we hit a whale just under the surface of the water that probably dove, or maybe a massive squid or something. At night time out in deep sea, you think of the stories about the old sailors where things would come up.

MARGARET Creatures from mythology?

SASHA Well, they've got such a vast area to grow big in.

MARGARET Also, at night your sight is much more fantastic.

SASHA You get phosphorescence and lights. Things do come by the boat to call and feed. If you dangle a flashlight in the water, you attract a whole bunch of creatures. Turn the light off, and then you watch. It looks like streaks of light where fish have come to feed and stirred up the water.

MARGARET Is it unusual for boats that small to cross the Atlantic by themselves?

SASHA Oh no. Anything is possible. Ours was 42 feet. I think you could probably go anywhere in the world these days, and if someone was listening to the radio, you could get rescued. Maréva's been taught how to use a flare gun, the radio, how to push the button on the emergency position relay beacon. If we're putting them in a situation where there's just the four of us, for example, then every one of us has to be able to help the other one—because I could be overboard, Paul could be in a state of shock or coma, and so why should we keep the kids ignorant about how to use the safety tools?

MARGARET Well, that's good. But it is a small space. Maybe it's because I'm from the prairies, I always think kids have to run wild through blocks and blocks and miles and miles. How did you contain them and keep them happy and not going crazy?

SASHA Whatever we did must have worked for our family. We sailed from Bora Bora, for example, directly to San Francisco. We didn't stop at Hawaii, because it would have added another two weeks to the trip. We got into San Francisco, and right ahead of us is one of these big American Safeway stores. They've got the donut shop, the ice cream, the jellies, probably a little electronic horse you could ride. I said to Aisha, 'Look at all the people, look at all the stuff, let's go!' And she said, 'No, I've got something I'm doing on board.' She hadn't touched land for a couple of months, and she wanted to finish up what she was doing. I thought, Are you nuts? [*laughs*] When she got up there, she was like a Martian or something. We put her in the grocery cart and she's saying, 'Look at all this stuff!'

MARGARET Tell me about a typical day when you were in the middle of the voyage.

SASHA Our day was a 24-hour day, because we always have someone on watch. It's less stressful for the family if you don't have an extra crew member, because otherwise we're worried about how he or she is doing.

MARGARET Like having a guest or something.

SASHA A relative. A typical day—I'd usually take the morning. I would've been up from 3:00 to 6:00 in the morning, but then I'd stay up to get breakfast going.

MARGARET Three to 6:00 would be your morning watch? At the wheel?

SASHA Yes, up on top when Paul was down. I'd make breakfast, and Maréva or Aisha would usually sleep through the night. We'd call Maréva if we had to do a sail change in the middle of the night, so she could take the wheel. Everybody slept with harnesses on. We always clipped on when we were on deck. This is understood. Or life-jackets for little kids. Then we'd make breakfast and everybody got together.

MARGARET What would you eat?

SASHA You don't just nibble on a bun. You look forward to meals. You put out a lot of energy, because your sleeping patterns are all broken up. I was in great shape—big muscles, no big belly, working, and the fresh air. [*laughs*]

MARGARET Could you store eggs?

SASHA Oh yes, eggs are amazing. They'll last three months. I didn't varnish them or dip them in oil. If they came in cardboard containers, we'd turn them over every couple of days. The big trip was outfitting—we always bought groceries for, say, three months before heading out, plus extra cans or rice—we showed Aisha how fragile the eggs were and gave her a felt pen, and she made a dot on top of each egg and closed the lid. Aisha's chore was to take a look every couple of days and turn the eggs over, so all the dots were up or down. That worked really well.

MARGARET So you could have eggs and you could—

SASHA Near the end, I'd just crack the egg in the bowl before I threw it into the meal. A food I never eat except at sea is corned beef out of the can, bought in bulk. We tried different brands, ranging from 29 cents a can to two dollars, and saw what we could live with. At the 29-cent level, you've got parts you don't even want to know about. [*laughs*]

MARGARET It's a bit like doggy food, isn't it? So corned beef hash and eggs … and rice.

SASHA Yes, and onions. Leftover rice would get turned into rice pudding or fried rice. I learned how to be creative with leftovers. And a big pot of tea or coffee, and juice, and snack time again probably around 10 o'clock.

MARGARET Getting back to your schedule, at 6:00, make breakfast, call them up for breakfast at 7:00—

SASHA Then Paul would start Maréva off on her school work. I'd go to bed and try and catch an hour or so.

MARGARET Who'd be at the helm?

SASHA Paul would be.

MARGARET Could he help Maréva at the same time?

SASHA Yes, we'd set her up and then, if she had any questions, Paul was there. Unless it was really bad weather.

MARGARET She would do that from 8:00 to 12:00?

SASHA We'd try blocking it in that way and try to make it work. Then if we had a—

MARGARET A rainstorm or something?

SASHA Not even that drastic. If we caught a fish, say, we'd stop and bring it in and have some out of it. If it was a nice day, we might start laundry, because you'd do a little bit, you know, whenever you could.

MARGARET But this is just your general ideal schedule.

SASHA Yes, an ideal schedule would be having Maréva study for the morning.

MARGARET Then lunch?

SASHA Yes, and I'd be up by that time. Usually I found that, when I lay down, I'd count to 10, or do 10 sit-ups, and I'd be out until I was called, or just wake up maybe three minutes before the switch-over ... So, lunch. The kids would get creative with couscous or canned fruit or custards where popular. I think we developed a bit of a sweet tooth. We found wonderful instant mashed potatoes done in Mylar packages from France—you could make 'em into hash browns or whatever. The kids would experiment. We learned how to make a kind of poor-man's chutney using a can of peaches and a little vinegar. We tended to experiment.

MARGARET Because you got sick of the blandness?

SASHA Yes, and longed for fresh stuff, which didn't tend to last very long. It was nice to buy green tomatoes, but usually in the store they were already red.

MARGARET Or could rot instead of turning red.

SASHA That would be one of the other jobs.

MARGARET 'Oh, my goodness, all the tomatoes are going, I think it's time to eat tomato, scrambled!'

SASHA Or tomato sauce for spaghetti, or a bean stew or something like that. One of the kids' jobs was to check the vegetables daily for mould. With oranges we learned a trick of wrapping them in newspaper, so if there was mould growing on one, it wouldn't contaminate the whole works.

MARGARET So you would lunch from noon to 1:00?

SASHA First, we'd do a sun shot for navigating—pick the sun right at its peak. It took about 20 minutes to figure out where we were on the chart, check the mileage. Then lunch. The kids helped out, depending on what slant we were living at. We have a propane stove and, if it was really sloppy, we'd always end up cooking with pots larger than the amount of stuff we needed to cook with.

MARGARET Because you were moving.

SASHA Yes, you always think of safety first. Burns at sea are really nasty to deal with, so we'd have sandwiches or cheese and crackers instead. It seemed like we were always munching. Then in the afternoon, we'd just generally look around and clean up, because there's a lot of salt spray on stuff, and it's really important to keep busy, for morale and to pass the time—not just busy work for the sake of keeping busy, but because things were always wearing out, because the boat was constantly moving.

MARGARET And you wanted to stay on top of it to prevent problems.

SASHA Really major ones, like rips.

MARGARET I'm sure there's a lot to do.

SASHA Just to keep it clean. Kids love to dust. We'd give them a little oiled rag and have them polish up the winch, or give them Windex bottles, just put water in them, they'd do the squeezie and wipe and polish. They loved that. Everybody helped out. I think that's the part about the family that's important, because it's a real team. I hope there's satisfaction—that they know we appreciate the work that's done. Like making beds, or rolling up stuff, oiling—we had an outboard motor strapped on the back, and Aisha would go with her oil gun, squeak it, and then pull it to make sure it was still going to start. Sometimes, too, we'd find as adults we were a little bit tired, on edge, because if we had to be up 24 hours, we were up 24 hours. That's what we had to do.

MARGARET You get tired from having to stay alert.

SASHA But you have to, see with kids—

MARGARET Kind of hyper-alert.

SASHA You have to be able to rest your body after that to bring it back to normal. The kids learned when to be quiet and when to help out. Maréva and Aisha would do a watch around dinner time, 5:00 to 6:00. Maréva said she could manage an hour, but we did a half hour with adult supervision, take a look around, check the compass heading, see if there were clouds building up or major changes in the water that might indicate winds coming, waves increasing, so we'd have time to prepare.

MARGARET Let's wrap up the day. After dinner, what then?

SASHA We'd get ready for bed. We'd have the radio on at night time. Actually, I would love to hit the sack, because I was on 9:00 to 12:00, and Paul would do 12:00 to 3:00, then I took over, 3:00 to 6:00. I'd say good night to the kids, brush my teeth, and do a wipe-down and make sure the kids were tucked—because, even stressed, you've got to keep normalcy, and the kids needed their routine. If I knew they were sleeping, I didn't have to worry about them.

MARGARET Children and boats like their routines.

SASHA So do adults.

MARGARET This is really switching gears here, from boats to life, but I keep wondering: When did you first want to have a baby?

SASHA I was up in Jervis Inlet, and we were at a Native Environmental Studies school. Paul and I had been married, oh, four or five years. I just decided I wanted a kid. We'd been married long enough. I knew him; he knew me. It was time. Then it didn't happen, and I was very disappointed. It wasn't until about a year later. It just sort of clicked on one day.

MARGARET Time.

SASHA I started thinking it would be nice to have my own. I felt old enough to be able to. I was glad I had the opportunity to choose. Compared to some other people for whom—oh my gosh, it just happened. I was looking forward to it, and we were set up. I got married at 21—it was awful, because my mom got me my wedding dress for my birthday present. [*laughs*] I wasn't too anxious to have children right away, because I felt so much like a kid myself. There were too many things I wanted to do first. At 27, it seemed like a better age—where I still had a lot of energy and patience. If you really want to be a mother—it means someone who is nurturing, understanding, helpful, and supportive.

That's a real job. I don't think sometimes people appreciate how much of a real job it is. Being there and yet not dominating that person. Being more a guide.

You read all the baby books and you think, Oh, I'm pregnant so [*laughs*] why don't I feel different? I should tell you this story, because it's kind of funny. I had one of those irregular periods, had been on birth control pills for years and went off, and we were sailing the boat down the coast, and I was thinking how really irritable I was sometimes, grumpy, and—What the hell was I doing? We were down in Southern California, and my period hadn't come, and I thought, No big deal, sometimes it's late, but then I began spotting, which threw me off. I thought, Cancerous lodes!

MARGARET Oh no!

SASHA And I'm in California, going to Mexico, and I said, 'Paul, I can't even say "blood" in Spanish let alone explain, my nipples are sore, they ache, they're swollen.'

MARGARET And you're still grumpy.

SASHA Grumpy! I thought I must be sick, so before we headed down to Mexico, I thought it would be best if I quickly went home—because we still had our medical insurance on line—and talk to a doctor.

MARGARET In English.

SASHA We'd heard horror stories about people not communicating properly and having the wrong organ cut out. I wanna go home! We hitch-hiked home in matching yellow raincoats and little packs. We were just going to zip up to Vancouver and say hi.

MARGARET Just get up there and have a pap smear!

SASHA Or get my leg cut off. [*laughs*] We'd stop and I'd say, 'Do you smell hamburgers?' Paul would say, 'We just had breakfast, we had coffee and toast, and it's only—what's your problem?' 'I'm starving,' I'd say. So we'd go to the truck stops, and I'd [*makes pig noises*]—and he's looking at me in amazement, because I was used to tea and a bun and off for the day, and then a good supper later. Thinking back, he remembers watching me savour even the ketchup, because it was food! [*laughter*] Finally we arrived. We didn't even go to my parents' place. I didn't want them to know we were here for something medical. I took my girlfriend aside confidentially and asked her for the name of a family doctor.

MARGARET Ta da da dum!

SASHA So the doctor does a test, comes back and says, 'Mrs. Dupré, there's nothing wrong with you except you're pregnant!' Oh! How do you wrap your brain around that? My girlfriend was ecstatic, because she was wondering whether I was going to die. We stopped and bought a bottle of champagne. This was about 10 o'clock in the morning. I got home and said, 'Excuse me,' to my girl-friend's husband, 'I have to talk to Paul,' and I just put this brown-bagged bottle on the table. If it's scotch or something, he knows I'm going to die, right? [*laughter*] Instead, there's a bottle of champagne, and I said, 'We're celebrating. We're having a baby.' He was really excited. Then I told my folks.

MARGARET Did you think, I'm going to change my life because I'm pregnant, or did you say, 'We're going to have children and we're going to take them in our boat and keep sailing'?

SASHA It was them coming into what we were doing as opposed to us adapting. I had to deal with the whole gamut of, 'Oh god, our grandchild'—Paul's mom is afraid of water, his father doesn't know how to swim. In fact, Paul can't swim. Most sailors can't. They figure if the boat goes down, they're not going anywhere.

MARGARET So you had to convince them.

SASHA There was this tearful, 'Are we ever going to see you again? You're not taking our grandchild out on the water?' [*laughter*] So we had to sit back. We both have families quite ensconced in society, thinking, Oh good, now Paul and Sasha will settle down. They'll sell the boat. So we came back and sold the boat. For a while they thought we'd seen the light and had matured, now that we were having children. Then we built a bigger one. I think there's a quiet respect growing …

MARGARET Over time.

SASHA Yes, they don't have to agree with what it is I'm doing, but the kids are always clean and well-behaved, and we seem happy.

MARGARET They're terrific kids. But maybe it would've happened even if you were in a suburban bungalow.

SASHA Oh, I think you make wherever you are work. If you decide that the family is important to you, then I think you'll try to take that into consideration. I've had to assess what my values are, how I feel about lying, or, oh, how I want to treat other people, or how I want them to see me. Or just respect. A lot of questions come up from the kids, or we see things maybe we wouldn't see if we stayed at home.

MARGARET People starving.

SASHA Yes. There was a fellow in a park in Portugal. We'd been there a couple of times to have lunch, because everybody had big barbecues there. He had an old dog, and he was drinking a lot, and we never saw him eat. We cooked up a bunch of food, and it was more than we could eat. We had fresh figs and fresh this and fresh that. This old guy was sitting over there. I said, 'Paul, we've got all this stuff left over, and we don't have a fridge. I don't want to just throw it out. There's someone there.' So I made up a paper plate and said, 'Maréva, would you like to go over?' Because we don't speak much Portuguese, we just motioned, Would he like some? It's not like, Oh, you're poor, have some food.

She said, 'Oh, mom, this is our food. I don't want to.' I said, 'Well, are you full? We've all had seconds. I don't want to chuck it out when there's someone else hungry. Why not put it on a plate instead of chucking it in the garbage hoping he'll scoop it out later?' Portugal doesn't really have a social program for its poor so everyone tries to help out amongst the community. She went over and ended up saying 'please' to him, and he took it and said, '*obrigado*,' thank you. That was it. She just came back, and it wasn't like, Oh look, now we fed that poor person. It's just like you do your thing. We had a talk about that when we went home, about trying to respect or help someone—we've got lots and would like to share.

Next day, we decided to stop in the park, and we just had a loaf of bread and some apples. We could smell all the grills, and it was like, Oh Paul, we'll send you off the market to get something, when this lady came over with a huge pan of barbecued sardines. Everybody had gotten together for an occasion, a birthday or something, and they just had too much food. 'It's hot, it's fresh, it's ready to eat now. Why waste it? Here, this is for you.'

MARGARET So it came round again.

SASHA We were treated. 'A good day to your family.' We brought her the pan back, all scrubbed and washed—that was Maréva's job to do. It's not that you expect every time you feed someone else, you're going to be given a meal down the road. It's just that we felt good about sharing, and that lady felt good about sharing and leaving it open, so that can happen. Instead of always just looking.

MARGARET Providing an environment that can allow these things to happen, and being aware of them.

SASHA Being aware.

MARGARET Did you ever sit down and work out how you wanted to raise kids, or is it something you figured out as you went along?

SASHA No, I think you have to have a bit of game plan.

MARGARET What was yours?

SASHA We wanted to be honest with them. I don't think you can ever tell them too much. To answer questions. We expect the kids to respect other people. When my parents say stop, that's the time to stop. Because if you're walking down the road or something, a parent might see an accident about to happen, and if their kid stops because you ask them to stop, you might prevent it. There isn't time to argue. A lot of that comes up on the boat.

MARGARET How about discipline? What is your and Paul's method of saying no, especially on a boat?

SASHA We believe that it's really important to be together. If something goes wrong, then it's not a matter of talking about it. You're told that this has to be here, and there's a reason for it, and you might forget it once, but that's where it's got to be. If the kid comes by and just goes *dump!* they have an opportunity to put it back. If that doesn't work, they're sent off on a quiet time, and they're not to rejoin us until they feel that their behaviour can change. That's been the rule.

MARGARET So your method is to separate.

SASHA That's been really effective for us. All of a sudden they're just going to their room—we don't even have a room sometimes, it'll be on your bunk!—and we have to ignore the screaming, if it's happening. You learn as an adult to keep your eye level up here, and that child doesn't exist until the child says, 'Okay, I'm sorry, mommy' or—everyone has differing abilities to think things out—Maréva would know to come to say, 'Okay, let's talk about it.'

The Stepmother
Coming In on Act Two

Sita Johnson, born in 1955 in Kampala, Uganda
Stepmother of two sons
Interviewed by Margaret Dragu

MARGARET At any point you can say, 'I changed my mind. This isn't for me.'

SITA I'll tell you what my reservations are. I'm a very verbal person, but I'm not sure I can really talk about my true feelings. Not because I'm afraid to. I'm concerned about how it would come across to people who know these kids—

MARGARET You want to protect your stepchildren.

SITA —who are not *my* family. For instance, I don't want to offend their mother.

MARGARET Or your mother.

SITA My mother is fairly aware of how I feel, so I'm not concerned really about the people who are close to me, who know. If they were my children, I would feel completely comfortable. When I'm talking about someone else's children, I don't feel as comfortable talking candidly.

MARGARET Maybe that's the whole thing about being a stepparent, or the second careperson. They don't call you 'stepmom' or 'mom,' they call you 'Sita.'

SITA Yes.

MARGARET Being the stepmother is an interesting position isn't it? Cinderella, Snow White. There's so much violence in Grimm fairy-tales. Stepmothers reach a terrible end. They're put in hot shoes or rolled in barrels with spikes. The stepmother's painted as an incredible ogre.

SITA [*laughs*] An ogre, and an incredible force.

MARGARET A *very* powerful force—because she's stolen the father's love—and the story is told from the child's perspective, so it's seen in Gothic terms. It's also to do with inheritance—where the blood line goes and where the money goes.

SITA The stepfamily situation is very complex. The dynamics are much more complex than I even imagined.

MARGARET And we're affected by this mythology even today. We're still walking around with Snow White.

SITA Right—and it's told from the child's perspective. The child, the stepchild, is painted as being, the most perfect, beautiful little being who does no wrong and is treated absolutely unjustly. It's the way I used to look at things, too. I totally sympathized with Snow White and Cinderella, and Hansel and Gretel. I would say I've changed my mind. I sympathize with the stepmothers now. [*laughs*] I understand. They were perhaps more wicked than they should've been, and they were extreme, because they acted on their impulses. I understand where those impulses came from, because there is a lot of jealousy, on both parts, I think—on the part of the stepchild and on the part of the stepparent. They're both trying to share one person, and it's not a natural relationship that you've grown up with. I had to share my dad with my mother and that was difficult at times, but basically that's all there was.

MARGARET The child is not innocent either. Children have no sense of logic or right and wrong. All these things have to be taught. They're physically violent and very manipulative, because they're trying to survive. These things are all natural and human. We might not like all of them, but they are in all of us, and, in kids, they're raw.

SITA Yes, and you're never told about what Snow White and Hansel and Gretel and the rest of them did to their stepmothers—how they interacted with their fathers, that drove their stepmothers crazy, and how the fathers reacted. That's the key. Even in a good relationship, if you're made to feel that you take second place to the children, no wife is going to enjoy or accept that—or at least no one who expects more and expects to be an equal partner. I think a lot of the feeling of, 'I wish they would go away, I wish they weren't here,' has nothing to do with the children themselves as people. It's much more to do with the relationship with the spouse.

MARGARET How does the relationship with the spouse

change when the children are in the picture?

SITA To start off, it's a different relationship. There is a lack of the privacy and the exclusivity that one expects in a new relationship. In a nuclear family, you marry someone who doesn't have a previous family that they bring into the new relationship. You start off on a much more even footing. In blended or stepfamilies, you never start out on an equal footing. Your status is quite different. You have to deal with the problems and feelings that are still unresolved from the previous marriage. You are coming in on Act Two.

MARGARET Was it a surprise to learn David had children?

SITA No, it wasn't a surprise, because I knew that he had twin boys. When I first met him and started dating him, they weren't around. They were with their mother, but I knew of their existence. I actually thought to myself, Well, I certainly don't want to marry a man with children, so I'll just go out with this fellow and have a good time. [*laughs*] Never thinking that I'd end up marrying him.

MARGARET What did you think it was going to be like, before you jumped in with both feet? Can you remember?

SITA Well, initially, I didn't think he was someone I would marry—because he had children—even though I thought he was a great person. It was one of the reasons I was not that interested, but then, of course, our relationship grew, and I became very attached to him, and fell in love, and then things started to change. It wasn't a typical courting, or similar to any relationship I'd had before, because I'd never been out with a man with children. It was much more difficult, much more complex, because of the presence of the twins.

MARGARET They must have come back at some point.

SITA They came back after two months, and that was a major shock. The reality. The shock was not that they came back, or that they were very important to him, but how much he changed once they were back.

MARGARET In what way did he change?

SITA Well, he ... he practically dropped me! We'd had a wonderful idyllic summer, like any courting couple when you first meet and you're in the rosy phase, and it often peters out with time or becomes more realistic. This just ended in a day—there was change in a single 24-hour period. With the kids around, I felt I was not important. I didn't really think he wanted to continue the relationship, even though he never said anything like that, but the way he behaved made me feel like that.

I was actually quite surprised that he continued calling and wanting to see me. But the kids came first, there was no doubt about that. Their schedule, their needs, everything was geared to them. He's a bit of an extreme even among single fathers, the children are the focus of his life and excessively important to him. For a long time that has been the case, that I've felt that their needs and their demands on him came first, and what anybody else in his life needed was second. Or last. Including in many cases his own needs.

MARGARET This change would be a shock to see in 24 hours.

SITA Yes. [*laughs*] It was a complete shock—even though I had anticipated that things would change, I didn't realize how much they would change.

MARGARET How old were the kids then?

SITA At the time, they were almost 10, about nine and a half. So they were young kids.

MARGARET When you first met them, how did that first meeting go? You must have been extremely nervous.

SITA [*laughs*] Yes, I think any person would be in that position. The first time I met them, they were very guarded and just sort of glared at me, stared at me, and didn't communicate with me.

MARGARET They knew you were dating their father?

SITA Yes. I don't know how much they knew. I don't know what David told them, but they knew that I was a woman in his life, so they were aware of that. It took a little while to feel comfortable with them and for them to feel comfortable with me. I really like children, so for me it wasn't a huge problem. I wasn't terribly afraid or threatened, although I found the two of them together, and being twins, a little scary, because they were always, and still are, extremely close and very united. Both looked at me with exactly the same eyes.

MARGARET It's a magic thing—twins.

SITA It's quite remarkable. I didn't know any twins growing up. I didn't realize how strong the relationship is between identical twins. It's been fascinating to watch their development. There've been some really wonderful things in terms of being involved in their lives. Partly just getting to know them as people, separate from all that's going on in the whole relationship and the dynamics, but also watching their quite incredible and wonderful relationship with each other, and watching it develop. Just watching them grow from 10 to 15 years has been fantastic.

MARGARET When you and David decided to get married, how did you tell the twins?

SITA Well, he told the twins. I think they still remember it. Perhaps it was the right thing to do, that he should tell them—they're his children—but sometimes I think that we should have told them together or discussed it with them together after that, and we really didn't. David told them, and they had to deal with it. That's when it was very difficult for a while. They had sensed that things were getting more serious. That's when the hostile behaviour came out.

MARGARET How did the hostile behaviour manifest itself?

SITA Oh, not talking to me, telling me that they didn't like 'strangers' in their house.

MARGARET And you were a stranger.

SITA After knowing them for two years. Two-and-a-half years. Suddenly, I was a stranger. 'And we don't like strangers in our house.' A number of things. They'd sit between us. One of them would take the lead generally. They'd just do what they could to get between us. At that age also, it was quite funny to watch in some ways, because they were so transparent. They were threatened by our closeness and our relationship. Some of it was a reflection of their mother's feelings as well. Because she was reacting in different ways. She actually turned out to be quite supportive when the time came, when we told her we were engaged. That's when I saw a change in the kids, in terms of their acceptance.

MARGARET They were still taking their cues from her?

SITA Very much so. At this point they were about 11.

MARGARET They were obviously frightened and feeling disempowered. Because they weren't part of the decision, I suppose.

SITA I'm really not sure. I don't have good insight into what they were feeling. I think a lot of it was that they thought they might lose their dad, even though we both reassured them that that wouldn't happen. Perhaps that was a fear. I don't really know, because I didn't get much from them in terms of explanation or verbal expressions of their feelings. It was much more physical expressions. [*laughs*]

MARGARET You were the only woman in that foursome.

SITA And still am.

MARGARET And women are more verbal and men are less so.

SITA Very much so.

MARGARET Boys even less so.

SITA I still have a problem with that. There are times when I want to sit down and discuss something, and all three of them look at me as if I'm mad. [*laughs*] That'll probably continue to be the case. Although they do listen, they don't respond very much. I'm learning to accept that that's just the way they are.

MARGARET What did you expect your role as stepmother to be?

SITA I didn't really know what the situation would be. When we were dating and decided to get married, they lived with their mother and spent approximately half the time with David. She and David had shared custody, like most stepfamilies I know.

MARGARET They only had to take a bus across the city to their mom.

SITA Right. Or they were driven there. Their main home was their mother's, where they spent a lot of time. Robert's home was theirs too, naturally. I expected that to continue, but after we were engaged, their mother made the decision to move away to another country. That changed everything. We had bought a house and moved in and had about two-weeks notice that she was leaving the country and that the kids were going to be with us. It was quite a time. I remember it very well.

MARGARET That's hard.

SITA Very hard. I had no say in this decision. It was imposed on me, and I didn't have a choice, and I felt it wasn't fair. We were just setting up home, and it was the first time that we had lived together, and I was getting ready for the wedding and having to arrange and organize all that and working full-time—and suddenly I was going to have these two kids as well. Part of me said, 'This is not fair.'

MARGARET That's a lot of change and a lot of responsibility.

SITA All at once, yes, it was a huge change. Change can also be very energizing and exciting. As it turned out, things worked out marvellously. When the kids arrived one morning with their little suitcases, I just took one look at them and said, 'How could I deny them this?' It was really good, in fact, that they were living with us full-time, because they felt that they were totally part of our lives—and they were part of the planning for our wedding. They were interested in what my bridesmaids were going to wear, what china I was choosing. It made the whole thing more fun for me, which you couldn't have convinced me of before they arrived. I thought, No way is this going to be fun. They were just great, and our relationship grew much stronger at that time. It was really good for us and has been great for our relationship throughout. Once they were living with us full-time and their mother was in another country, they felt they had permission to like and accept me. Usually stepfamilies are a shared situation, and couples don't have the chance to have the kids full-time in their home. I think that's actually harder for the kids.

MARGARET Yes

SITA My parents had been concerned about the difficulty of my situation as a stepmother. I was very aware of it, too. I certainly didn't go into it lightly—it took me about two years to decide. [*laughs*]

MARGARET But you obviously thought about it as much as you could.

SITA With as much experience as I felt I had. It still doesn't prepare you.

MARGARET No, whether for biological or non-biological parenting, you can't be prepared. I'm convinced.

SITA I was raised in a very traditional nuclear family, but also with a large extended family. Which is quite different from the experience that my stepchildren have had. I was born in Uganda, I was the eldest child, the first. I grew up with lots of love and also lots of discipline—an absolutely marvellous way to grow up, even though I may not have liked it at the time.

MARGARET How many relatives did you have around you to form that extended family?

SITA This was all my father's family, because they were all in Uganda. My mother's family was in India, and I was not very close to them, very familiar with them, but my father's family was very close. I had a grandmother, and I could spend time at the homes of my aunts and uncles and feel completely comfortable. My stepchildren don't have this luxury, they aren't used to dealing with a lot of adult relatives.

MARGARET How many aunts and uncles were in Uganda with you?

SITA My father comes from a family of eight kids—four boys and four girls—so he had three brothers and four sisters.

MARGARET Did they have children?

SITA No. I was the only one initially, because I was the eldest grandchild. They had children later.

MARGARET You were the princess.

SITA Yes, definitely, I was the little pearl [*laughs*]

MARGARET And you're still close, your family.

SITA Oh, we're very close, and probably getting closer. A lot more came to my wedding than I would have expected, or they sent telegrams. David and I visited them, too. They live all over the world. My own family had to leave Uganda in 1972. I came to Canada in '73 when I was 18. Here, we were a very nuclear family without an extended family.

MARGARET Did your background affect how you saw your role as a stepparent?

SITA I thought I would be a nice adult in my stepchildren's life, like a genial aunt—who would not be a parent, because they have two very loving and very devoted parents—but someone who would spoil them a bit. Give them treats, and yet contribute in some way to their lives.

MARGARET That sounds perfect.

SITA It does. It's not the role that I found myself in.

MARGARET What is the role?

SITA Partly because their mother is in another country, I'm in a more parental role than I expected to be.

MARGARET What does that mean to you?

SITA When we were married, these children initially lived with us for a few months, and then their mother took them to live with her for two years, and we only saw them for a few weeks at a time on holidays—Christmas, Easter, summer. It was good for our marriage, as we had some space and time for ourselves. Our relationship changed during that time as well.

MARGARET And with David, too?

SITA Yes. He missed them terribly. He found it very difficult to be separated from them and so uninvolved in their daily lives. I imagine that's what their mother is feeling now, because last September they came back to live with us. Full time. They spend the holidays with her now. Our relationship changes all the time. When they lived with their mother, I really was like a third party in their lives. We had some difficult times.

MARGARET During this time they would be coming for just a holiday?

SITA Just for the holidays. I always found it difficult. They hadn't seen their dad for a while. They were very possessive of him, very demanding. He responded to that, naturally. I felt left out. Even though I could understand it, it was hard. I was left out in many cases. Or I felt unimportant in their trio. The kids completely monopolized his attention—they're very good at that! You know, they took it out on me. That was very hard. Even though I cared about them and was very fond of them, it was very hard to be on the receiving end. That's something I don't think that David understands.

MARGARET It doesn't make it hurt less even if you understand.

SITA That's right. When they first lived with us, I found I was in a more nurturing role, which I enjoyed. They were younger and still needed a mother. They needed someone to run their baths and take them for haircuts and talk to them and cuddle them a bit. Now that they're older, 14, they just turned 15, my role is actually quite different from that initial period, which I found very rewarding. They still need nurturing from their mother; they don't accept it from me. What they do need is structure, discipline, guidance. I don't feel as comfortable with that, particularly disciplining them. I have a real problem with that.

MARGARET Very difficult to discipline unless you have complete authority.

SITA And unless you feel completely comfortable.

MARGARET Even then it's still hard.

SITA It's still hard. [*laughs*] People I know who have teenagers find it difficult, so I realize it's difficult dealing with teenagers anyway.

MARGARET The difficulties must be underscored, for a stepparent.

SITA It's very difficult. I've often felt that if they were my own natural children, I'd feel much freer disciplining them. Actually, I'm much more careful with them than I would be with my own children, where I would feel free to say, 'Stop it,' or 'That's enough,' or whatever.

MARGARET To provide the boundaries. This is where you have to weigh what their mother does, what their father does, see if it's in keeping.

SITA I tiptoe much more—although I have to say, basically they're very good kids. I'm not talking about them running off and stealing cars, or not coming back home, and things like that. They're very self-disciplined.

MARGARET Lucky you!

SITA Yes, I am lucky, although they watch far too much TV, and we don't want them to, so that's an issue. Some of it is in the way they communicate. They will be defiant and rude.

MARGARET Teenage sullen.

SITA Right, which one expects from teenagers, but one doesn't want to encourage that style of communication.

MARGARET Not fun to receive it.

SITA No, and then there are other, probably less important things, but things that matter to me, like courtesy, respect for other people, table manners even. I decided table manners are definitely not the most important thing, and I have to let go of my standards a little bit, but things like treating us and each other with respect, and being courteous to other people—that type of thing is important. Boundaries need to be set about behaviour, what they are and aren't allowed to do. I'm basically strict.

MARGARET Noise, that kind of thing? Bumping, yelling, slamming?

SITA To mention a few.

MARGARET Now I want to ask you about the idea of having a baby. How old are you?

SITA Thirty-five.

MARGARET Thirty-five. Still young.

SITA Getting older every day. [*laughs*]

MARGARET Everybody is! How does that fit into the scheme of the ultra-blended family that you are in now?

SITA David and I would like to have a child. We decided that before we got married, because that was an important issue for me, that if he did not want more children and did not want to raise another child, I did not think I could sacrifice my desire to do that. But we did discuss it and it was something we both wanted. He had much more trepidation about it than I did because he's raised —

MARGARET He's been there before.

SITA That's right! Yes, and I think I have a much more idealistic view of having or raising a child than he does. We decided to wait a little while, because we felt we all needed time to adjust to the situation.

MARGARET Have you talked about it with the twins?

SITA We haven't. We've informed them. We haven't really discussed it or asked their opinion. We felt it was really a decision between the two of us—that their opinion probably wouldn't affect our decision—but we have told them that's what we plan and want.

MARGARET That it's a possibility.

SITA That it's a possibility. They actually brought it up before we did, because we just sort of avoided talking to them about it.

MARGARET Good on them. Now you're very successful and respected by your peers as a speech pathologist.

SITA My career is established sufficiently that I'm not really worried about taking time off. What worries me is that I'm so used to being a career person and having so much structure in my life, that to stop all that and have an infant and follow them around scares me a bit. Even though it's something I look forward to. I don't really know what I'll do. I've decided that I'll wait and see how I feel. I may feel that I really have to get to work for my own sanity after three months or six months, but at this point in time I would like a longer time with my child, and at home, without having the stress of work and other things.

MARGARET Do you think, being a speech pathologist, you'll learn from your own child?

SITA Well, I really enjoy watching my friends' children. I'm sure it'll be even more fun.

MARGARET And you also enjoy your stepchildren.

SITA I'm very lucky, because they are great kids. I knew that from the start, or I don't think I would've made the commitment to David. They have a lot going for them. They're smart, athletic, good-looking, they speak a few languages, and they are very well-travelled.

MARGARET Good senses of humour.

SITA And they have a wonderful relationship themselves.

MARGARET All that's healthy stuff.

SITA I think it has been fantastic for them. In many ways I feel lucky to have them in my life. I find them very interesting and wonderful to be with at times. There are also times when I wish they would just go away. Which ultimately they do.

MARGARET You can also develop real anger towards the spouse for not understanding that a child who comes with a partner can exclude you. It's a big stress in the whole family politic.

SITA In fact, my anger has been directed, perhaps unfairly, more at my husband than at the children.

MARGARET Because he's an adult.

SITA I do get angry at my husband for not understanding sometimes, sometimes at his ex-wife for interfering, and sometimes at the children, just for being there. But it's not at them for who they are as people, it's their presence. It's an intrusion on our privacy as a couple.

MARGARET And even wonderful parents are human, which means there's anger.

SITA Absolutely. The best parents, the most well-adjusted parents, have their off days. Kids can also really trigger that. [*laughs*] Play up to it. Provoke it.

MARGARET They can really push those buttons.

SITA They know how better than anyone else does. Sometimes, being a stepparent, I've had to remind myself that some of what goes on is not unique to the relationship.

The kids live with us now, and we are all getting used to each other—so our relationship grows closer all the time. We feel like a family and interact on that basis most of the time. I enjoy it now, but it's taken time, and effort, and patience, to get there.

Coping With Gotham

Black and Poor In Brooklyn

Martinique Somers, born in 1960 in Brooklyn, New York
Mother of Darcy and Jason
Interviewed by Susan Swan

SUSAN You have two kids of your own. How old are they?

MARTINIQUE My son Jason is six, and my adopted daughter Darcy is 14. She's my niece; her father abandoned her and I took her in. I'm 31. I also look after my mother's 11-year-old godchild, Tara, and a friend's two-year-old, Dalton. This apartment is very hectic, because a lot of people live here.

SUSAN How many?

MARTINIQUE I'm not saying.

SUSAN Seven, eight? It looks like a very spacious apartment. You have four bedrooms in a rent-controlled building in Brooklyn's Park Slope area.

MARTINIQUE I don't know, there's always somebody. I mean, it's my mother's place and she doesn't care. My uncle recently came to stay. He was into drugs, the whole works, and he, I guess, just got tired of his life, and he just showed up here about a month ago. So he's here. My brother is also here. I don't know if you'd call him a recovering addict, but he has never gotten himself together.

SUSAN He's a crack addict?

MARTINIQUE He was a crack addict. At one time he was really heavily into drugs and cocaine. My grandmother is the backbone of our family, so she always helped with the males. Liked to push them into whatever kind of projects they wanted to do. Since my grandmother's not here, he just doesn't do anything with himself. Luckily, two weeks ago he enrolled in a school to become a nurse's aid. That's progress, right? So he lives here, and my mother—but she's rarely here—me, and my two children, and my mother's godchild. She's 11. My mother has custody of her, but I raised her.

SUSAN Do you remember getting a sense from your mother about what it meant to raise children? Was it something that was a duty, or something fun? Was it a mixed blessing?

MARTINIQUE I didn't get any ideas from my mother. My mother is a workaholic—she's always worked. My mother just turned 52 and she celebrated her 25th anniversary of her job. She's a supervisor for a house insurance company in Manhattan. But you know, I don't think she ever fulfilled her dream—the house, kids, the husband who was really there. She had a steady boyfriend with us in the house until I was 16, but I never liked him or formed a bond with him. It was my grandmother who was my foundation. Now, my mother may disagree with that, but I relied on my grandmother for everything. From the day I was born, I always felt grandma was my second mom. My mother was never home with us. When we were older we were latchkey kids.

SUSAN How old was your mother when she had you?

MARTINIQUE She was 20 years old and she married my father and had me. The next year she had my brother. Right after that they separated and have been separated for all these years. She's not remarried. I don't have much of a relationship with my father. If he was to walk down the street, I probably wouldn't even recognize him. You see, my mother didn't have the time or energy to give me the input I needed. That's probably the reason I'm overweight. [*laughter*] I go to a lot of counselling for help in dealing with me and my kids.

SUSAN Are you close to your mother?

MARTINIQUE No. Basically, when I was four to five, I lived with my grandmother. She took all the grandchildren on a vacation, and when I came back, my mother had been in a car accident, and I didn't recognize her, I wouldn't go with her. So, nobody forced the issue, you know. I think a child between the ages of three and four needs a role model, and I didn't get that from my mother.

SUSAN You felt chronically frustrated?

MARTINIQUE When I think back, I don't really know what kind of child I was. I wasn't a loner, but I had my own thoughts and my own ideas, and I always felt like an old person. My mother could never understand that or deal with it.

SUSAN You had an old soul.

MARTINIQUE Maybe.

SUSAN Let's talk about you and mothering. You have decided to stay at home with your children, and you make a living looking after other people's children. Why?

MARTINIQUE Well, when I was a teenager, I always worked in summer jobs at youth camps, and I always seemed to be attracted to kids who people didn't like. I could always get along with the kids who other people don't have time for. So I've had a good rapport with children all my life. I'm the mothering type, you know.

SUSAN Yes, I can tell that about you.

MARTINIQUE When I got older, I worked at daycares and, after I had my son, I wanted to be home with him all the time. I don't like to leave him with anyone, even though I watch children. Even with these kids, the ones I watch, I tell their parents—if you can stay home, stay home. I'm doing it the opposite of my mother, no matter what the consequences are.

SUSAN Is money a problem for you? Do you get subsidy?

MARTINIQUE No. Money is a problem for me. Everybody says to me they don't know how I make it, but something always turns up. [*laughter*] That's how I live. As long as my kids are well dressed—as long as I know my son looks good, he's clean, he's neat, and he has, you know, basic clothes. Of course, no matter what you buy kids, they always want something different—but people give me things, and I just always find a way, even with my daughter Darcy, although I get no money from her father. He has a very good job, but …

SUSAN He gives you no money?

MARTINIQUE Oh no, no.

SUSAN Is welfare very strict in terms of what you can do and can't do once you get subsidy?

MARTINIQUE Welfare, it just becomes your life, it becomes like your man. [*laughter*] I'm never going on welfare, never! So many people I know are on it, and it's like they're constantly going down there with all these papers, and if this isn't right or whatever, then the welfare people cut you off. Who could live, knowing, 'This is all I get, this is my only income. If they cut me off, what am I going to do?' I don't want to be constantly bowing down to a master of any kind. That's not my style.

SUSAN Right now you are watching only one child for money?

MARTINIQUE Yes. Sometimes I get depressed over my financial problems, because I'm budgeting everything out, and then the kids will tell me, 'Well, we've gotta have this money for school and that money for school,' and I'm like, Oh, my god, where's it going to come from? But hey, it always winds up coming, and you do what you have to do. I'm very upfront and honest with my children, I say, 'Look, we can't afford to go out and get 16 boxes of cereal that no one's going to eat.' So we have to make a unit decision on what kind of cereal we're going to eat, little things like that.

SUSAN Is cereal an issue?

MARTINIQUE [*laughter*] Not really, but I use that as an example, because sometimes, it really is frustrating, you look at the price of these cereals—$4.09—'Okay, you really want it for sure?' 'I really want it, I have to have it.' [*laughter*] So I realize, okay, I'll buy it. Then it sits up there on the shelf and I get so mad. I tell them, 'You know there's kids out there who don't have cereal in the morning, there's children out there who don't get a decent lunch.' I send my son's lunch every day when he can't get a free lunch at school. I prefer to send it. Then he'll come home, and he doesn't eat half the things. I get so mad at him.

SUSAN How do you budget?

MARTINIQUE I can't tell you the last time I've been to a movie theatre, because in order for me to go, it's seven dollars now for adults, some places it's three or four for children, so, it's over 20 dollars. Then you have to buy stuff in the theatre, about which I've become very resourceful. I will bring my own popcorn. I'm not embarrassed. [*laughter*] We will bring a big pitcher of Kool-Aid, and we will bring our own candy.

SUSAN Great idea.

MARTINIQUE Yes. In Park Slope, there's the Park Slope

paper, there's the downtown Brooklyn paper. You just pick them up for free anywhere on the avenue. There are a lot of events in this city that you don't have to pay money for, and that's what we do. We pack our knapsacks, and put our sandwiches in there, and we go, and it only costs us our car fare. Which is a lot, too, but hey. I have some friends who work for Transit, sometimes I get block tickets—there's always a way. Not that you want to be a con artist, but you have to know how to deal with the system. Some things you have to lie about. It's very expensive to live.

SUSAN What would be something that you would lie about, for instance?

MARTINIQUE Well, now the new thing is about getting on the bus. My son is relatively tall, so they've been bugging me about paying for him since he was four years old. I refuse. I will get off the bus. Anyway, you have to lie a lot, I tell them my son is only five [*laughter*] if they make an issue. Most times, bus drivers are nice, they don't care. Some of them are very nasty, they will give you such a hassle.

SUSAN Is there a bus into Manhattan from Park Slope?

MARTINIQUE Yes, there's a bus into Manhattan. My mother takes it. You've got to take this bus, number 67, get off, and then go straight to Manhattan—I forget the name of the bus—it goes to the Wall St. area, at least.

SUSAN So you take that, when you can.

MARTINIQUE I don't go into Manhattan that much. The last time I was in Manhattan was Christmas. We go to 34th Street to see the tree and Macy's and the whole works—you know what I'm saying—so I'll go up then, and it's like, Oh my god, I get down in the subway, and I just get sick. I'm afraid of trains. I'm afraid I'm going to fall. [*laughter*]

SUSAN Fall off?

MARTINIQUE I don't know why, I'm standing on the stands, and the train pulls in, and I do get on, but I have a fear of trains. I have a fear of escalators.

SUSAN It's a common fear.

MARTINIQUE I have a fear of escalators. I will go into a building, and if there's no elevator, I'll ask if they have stairs. I can't go into some stores because they only have an escalator.

SUSAN What do you think is the biggest problem in your life with the children?

MARTINIQUE No time for yourself.

SUSAN No time for yourself.

MARTINIQUE During counselling they said that I don't see myself as separate from my kids. They say my kids are me and I am me, but it's like one entity. They're all clinging to me, and I get so involved in their lives. That's one thing that I've been trying to work out, because I don't have time to do anything for myself. There's always something that I have to do for them. A month ago, I decided I was going to read and I didn't care. If I go sit in the bathroom, they'll come in with me. If I go take a bath, someone's in there saying so and so and so and so. I feel like, Oh, my god. So I just said that I was going to read this book, and I got so into the book. Everybody was mad because I was reading, and there was no time for them, and I was like, I don't care what you do, I gotta read this last chapter. [*laughter*] I could not put the book down. Finally, one night, I just stayed up and finished the book when the kids were asleep.

SUSAN What was the book?

MARTINIQUE The book was *Sweet Whispers, Brother Rush;* it's a great book about a teenage girl who falls in love with a ghost.

SUSAN I wanted to ask you about the problems in Brooklyn. For instance, children are being killed here by stray gun-fire, and many kids are on drugs. How do you cope with that? Do you worry about your kids?

MARTINIQUE I worry about the kids a lot, but living in Park Slope is such a different environment. Being a Black person, I know both sides, even though I've lived here the majority of my life. My grandmother lived in Bedford Stuyvesant, for instance. Over there, people are always on the corner, sitting here, sitting there. A wino is your child's best friend. A junkie's your child's best friend. But over here, you see we have trees, we have parks, you know what I mean, so they don't get the input of everything. Sometimes I say, 'Oh my god, look, this child was killed by a bullet'—it could happen in Park Slope, we know that. We're not excluded. But it's a different environment, especially for Black children. Most Black kids don't live in this sort of area, and they don't have a chance to get away from it, so I feel that my kids are lucky. Darcy can't hang out up there at night the way I did when I was a teenager. I wouldn't let her go up there. Every time you look around, somebody is raped up there.

SUSAN When you say 'up there,' what do you mean?

MARTINIQUE Prospect Park. There's a lot of homosexuality, the negative kind, up there, people engaging in sex up there, people getting shot up there, people getting just whatever, harassed, for no reason.

SUSAN I thought, coming here this morning, What a nice neighbourhood this is. What a good place to grow up. The tree-lined streets are very pleasing to the eye.

MARTINIQUE It is, it is. It's very pleasing, and it's very serene. You hear about robberies, cars, every day someone's car is getting stolen, you hear about people getting shot. Now you're up here, on 8th Avenue, the further down the hill you go, the worse it gets. When you get down to 5th Avenue, it's a whole different thing. That's where the real life is. Up here it's like being in the country. I call it Staten Island, because it's so remote. The drugs are also here, but you don't see it, people live a different way.

SUSAN Have any of your children been involved in drugs?

MARTINIQUE No, thank god, no. I'm very honest and frank with them, and I said—when I was young, I did drugs, you know, I did marijuana, I did cocaine, I've done pills, all that kind of stuff, I drank incessantly—and I tell them about that. So they can learn to just say no. They always say, 'Oh, but you smoke.' I do smoke obsessively, and I tell them that, well, 'If you want to smoke, there's nothing I can say.'

SUSAN What about discipline? How do you discipline your kids, or do you discipline them? How does it work?

MARTINIQUE I punish, and I tell them the reason why. When I was a young person, I always said, If I have children, I would never hit them—because my mother didn't hit me that much, not so it really hurt, but she would slap me. Wow, and I was like,

Oh, my god, don't ever slap me in my face. But sometimes the kids get so out of hand.

SUSAN I know that well.

MARTINIQUE I'll hit them, you know, a little, and I don't use my hand. I'll get a real weapon.

SUSAN You'll get what?

MARTINIQUE [*laughter*] A strap, 'a weapon,' I said, but I mean like a strap, or something like that, you know. But—

SUSAN You say you'll get a strap. You have a strap.

MARTINIQUE I have a strap. Oh, yes, but that's mostly for threat, you know what I mean? I'll take it and I'll crack it like that, crack it like—pull it, hit it against something. 'Now you don't want that,' I tell them. 'Oh my god, that's gonna hurt.' I'm like, 'Don't lie to me, I don't like it when you lie,' and then they think I have this gift for knowing everything. I really don't. [*laughter*] Maybe I do a little bit, but they say, 'God, no matter what we do, you know, you know.'

SUSAN You were saying that the strap is mostly a threat, and you don't really like to use it. Can you give me an example of a time when you did feel a child deserved to be strapped?

MARTINIQUE Oh yes. In January, Darcy took money from me, some money and tokens. I knew she had taken it, because she's the only one who knows where I hide things. She came home that day, and I questioned her about it, and she got really defensive—she's like, 'No, no,' and so on—I was giving this child two dollars a day because she went to junior high school, and they want to eat out—anyway, she said, 'No, I didn't take it,' so I told her, I said, 'Take off your clothes!' [*laughter*] This is a learned behaviour. Anything you did wrong, my grandmother or my mother would always say, 'Get those clothes off you! You're going to get the strap.' I told her to get off her clothes. As she took off her pants, money fell to the floor. I can look back now and laugh, but in January, I didn't laugh about this. There's a kid's baseball bat over there in the plants [*laughter*], a little kid's baseball bat. I ran back there, and I got the bat, and I said, 'You're going to get it. I'm going to whack your behind, I'm going to beat you there.' I was so mad.

SUSAN Did she admit to stealing the money?

MARTINIQUE She swore she didn't take the money. I said, 'Where did this money come from?' She started talking about how she found it, she went into this whole long thing. Finally, I was so upset over the whole incident, I was almost on the verge of tears, I was holding my head down, and she ran out of the house. She ran away. I didn't know what to do. I called my counselling service. I said, 'Darcy ran off,' blah blah blah. And they in turn said, 'Oh, don't worry, she might have gone to a friend's house to cool off.' I said she never ran out of the house before. I've never had to deal with a runaway.

SUSAN Where did she go?

MARTINIQUE It turned out she went to the counselling service. She told them, not that I had threatened her with a bat, but that I had hit her with this bat, and that I always hit her, with bats, sticks, whatever, whatever. She just made up all this stuff. I was really hurt, because I usually put her on punishment when she disobeys me. I rarely hit her. I'd talked all this out with Darcy before, so she knew my policy here.

SUSAN It sounds like she must almost believe that you would hit her, because she was so used to being hit before she came to live with you?

MARTINIQUE No, that wasn't it at all. The threat was there, the threat was serious, and I told her that, yes, I would have hit her with that bat, okay? Because she doesn't take money from me and then lie over it. But that was a special occasion, when I lost my temper. I went down to the counselling centre and talked it over, just like I am talking with you. They asked me what happened. I told them and I said, 'I've been going to counselling with this child every week for three years.' I said, 'There were one or two occasions that I hit her, with my hand or something like that.' I'd told the counsellor I felt bad about this. Then the counsellor told Darcy she was acting like a spoiled rotten kid. She just felt frustrated if she didn't get her way. She thinks she can do whatever she wants. She's 14 now. That age is very hard.

SUSAN When you say you'd hit her, before, a couple of times, was that like a slap on the cheek or a cuff on the bum?

MARTINIQUE One day she went to camp and didn't come home until late. I had to go out looking for her. My friends were frantic—they had to go out looking for me now, because I was looking for her. When she finally waltzed in at 8:30 at night, she made up a long story: she had a nosebleed at camp and they told her to stand in front of the campsite. I had been there, and there was nobody at the camp. I made her come upstairs and remained outside to calm myself down. Then I said, 'Get your clothes off,' and I got the strap, and she was trying to get away, and I held up my arm, and I whacked, and I whacked, and I whacked.

SUSAN You whacked her bum?

MARTINIQUE Oh, I whacked her behind. That's why I wanted her to take off her clothes.

SUSAN I see.

MARTINIQUE She told the truth after that. That she had gone to a friend's house. I said, 'What kind of friends do you have, that they let a 12-year-old come to their house and they don't call the parents?' But people are different. I wouldn't let it happen, but some people are different.

SUSAN What was the other incident?

MARTINIQUE I can't remember. It was something trivial. Like I told the counsellor, I don't hit her regularly, because punishment is much better. She doesn't like to read, so I make her read, or give me an apology—and it has to be written.

SUSAN A written apology? Is that what you mean by punishment?

MARTINIQUE A written apology—you put down why you feel that you have to lie to me, why you do this and that. She doesn't like to write. I love to write, so I have her sit down and I say, 'Well, you write it, you think about it. You have the whole weekend to think about it. I want something really nice, I want to be able to believe it when I read it, okay? I don't want you to stand and tell me, I'm so sorry, I'm so sorry. No, you write it.' Sometimes I tell them, 'You can't play Nintendo, you can't watch TV.' Or, 'No, lady, you're in the house, you're on punishment, you're not going anywhere, and you're not watching TV, so you'd better find something to do. You're not reading too well, get a book out, read, draw, do something constructive. Otherwise I'll give you some chores to do. It's up to you.'

SUSAN And your son? What about punishment for him?

MARTINIQUE That's why they get mad at me. They say I don't do it. [*laughter*]

SUSAN You don't punish your son?

MARTINIQUE I've started, I've started a little bit with him, and I'll tell him—he has a little friend that he plays with outside, and he came and told me that, 'Martinique ...'—they all call me by my name—'Martinique, Henry was going to threaten me with a knife.' Then, my little girl said, 'Martinique, Jason was lying. Henry wasn't threatening him with a knife. They had a little spat outside.' So I picked up the phone and called a friend —I said, 'Hello Bob, this is Martinique.' I'm holding the phone, and Jason is listening. I say, 'I just wanted you to know that your son Henry threatened Jason with a knife, and I don't like that, and I'm so upset,' and so and so and so. Then Jason admits he didn't do it.

SUSAN He owned up.

MARTINIQUE He's waving his hands. I told him he was on punishment from the next day. He went to school, he came home, and he's getting ready to go outside, you know—well he's not that little, but you know, he forgot—so I said to him, he's changing his clothes, I said, 'Where are you going, where are you going?' He says to me, 'I'm getting ready to go outside.' I say, 'Oh, no. You lied to me, and you made someone look really bad. You're not going outside, you're being punished.' He goes on a lot of play dates with friends, I mean, it's every day.

SUSAN Play dates are arranged because the kids just can't go out on the streets?

MARTINIQUE Yes, true, and the parents will call and will say, 'Can Jason have a play date with my son,'—and it's good for him, because he doesn't have a dad as a role model. A lot of the boys, they have their dads, and they take him to the park, and they ride their bikes, and they do things like that.

SUSAN Where is Jason's father? Was he an important man in your life, or was he just a casual person?

MARTINIQUE No, he wasn't a casual person. He's not worth talking about.

SUSAN No?

MARTINIQUE I'll get too upset.

SUSAN Okay.

MARTINIQUE I don't even know where he is, and Jason doesn't know where he is. I tell him that he has a father—everybody has a father—but some kids don't have a dad. [*laughter*] A dad is someone who loves you, but fathers are someone who created you.

SUSAN Oh, that's a good distinction.

MARTINIQUE Yes, you know, that's how I make them distinct. Even this girl back here, Tara, her mother didn't know who her father was. Because she had a lot of men at that time. Tara goes to Catholic school, and they told her that she didn't have a father.

SUSAN May I ask you a question about the stereotype of Black families—that the women hold them together, and the men come and go and don't take very much responsibility. Do you think that stereotype is true?

MARTINIQUE It's very true. It's sad, but it's so true. My aunt recently said that she blames my grandmother for the downfall of all the men in our family. I don't blame her. There's a Black author, I don't remember his name, but he said on a talk show that Black women raise their daughters, but they love their sons. That is so true. I can look at my family and see that. You raise your daughter, from a little girl, you teach them. This is the way you do this, do that, you can have a doll. You take care of the baby, you do this and that and that. You don't do that with a son. And I was like, God, that's so true—I'm trying to be different.

SUSAN Just like you were saying, Darcy feels that you are easier on your son than on her.

MARTINIQUE Right. But it's not really true. You know, I tell them about age. Age differences really matter. I said, 'Darcy, when you were that age, I would not have put a lot of pressure on you, okay? When you were that age, I would not have given you chores.' I said, 'He has a chore, he makes up his bed. He sweeps the bedroom floor, that's a chore. That's something to show him that he lives in a family, everyone has responsibilities, okay?'

SUSAN So this is something you feel you're addressing in your own home. But you think the stereotype is true.

MARTINIQUE Oh, definitely. The stereotype is true. There's always that missing link. In many Black homes there is no father figure, so the mother, she's doing the best she can for all her children, but she has to be both mother and father for her boys. I used to get so upset about my son, because even though my brother lives here, I don't feel that he's a positive role model for my child. He's my brother, I love him, but he's not what I'm looking for. Therefore, you have to seek outside the home for these role models. A girl's going to have that, she's going to be with her mom, so it doesn't matter to her, but that boy, he's already missing something in his whole being, because at three and four he didn't have a dad. Unless you get right back into another relationship.

SUSAN And maybe, as you say, the mother feels a little sorrier for the boy, because he doesn't have the father figure.

MARTINIQUE He doesn't have it. Look at the men in my family. It's not only my brother, my uncle. This is my cousin, my brother has just turned 30. My uncle is 32. I have another cousin who is 31, the same age as me. I have another one who's 25. These are all men, okay? They're all the same. No one has a job. No one has any intention of getting a job, they all live at home with their mothers, because mom didn't instil in them the need to go out, to achieve something. I'm not talking about dumb men. These are men who are intelligent. My uncle went to college. He's had his own businesses. But, when they fail, hey, they come to their mothers. And he has a wife and kids.

SUSAN My last boyfriend was a Black writer, and he still lives at home.

MARTINIQUE You know what I'm saying? There's nothing wrong with it, but I feel that that's what it is. I told my grandmother, 'I'm going to try to break the stereotype. I'll go out there and get him a Big Brother, anything I have to do, to instil something in him.' I've taught him how to braid hair. Why? Because I tell him, 'Who's saying that your wife is going to be a good mother? Who's saying that, okay? Who's saying that you get married this week, and you have a baby, and so and so, that your wife might not die in pregnancy?' I tell him all that. 'She may die, she may run away from the family,' I say, 'I don't want to take care of your child, okay? You have to be responsible for yours. So, therefore, you have to learn how to braid the hair, comb the hair, groom them, take care of the body.' My daughter, the oldest one, went through her menstrual recently. He's learning about that. Why not?

SUSAN Good for you.

MARTINIQUE You know what I'm saying. Why do you hide these things? Why keep everything a secret? We're not ashamed of our bodies in our home. If you surround it with shame, they always want to go out and find out, well, what do breasts look like? Anything you hide from kids, they want to do and see. My mother was not open about anything. Everything was a secret.

SUSAN It creates an instant glamour and curiosity. What about the job of mothering itself? Do you think it's fair, the way women do all this work without getting paid for it or having it really acknowledged? Do you have any idea about how it could be better for women like yourself?

MARTINIQUE It's sad. Women don't get the praise. There was a talk show on, and the man was talking about how he wanted his wife to go back to work. She has three kids, and it's like, god, she has little ones, a newborn—two months old—and a three-year-old and a five-year-old. And I wondered, in that whole day, does he realize what this woman does?

SUSAN That's a good question.

MARTINIQUE Does he really realize? I wish I could have called Oprah and said to him, 'Do you really realize what she does?' If he was to stay home for one week, with those kids, would the house remain clean? Would he be able to bring a friend home from work and dinner be served on the table?

People don't understand what you have to go through.

SUSAN That's true.

MARTINIQUE My friends who work outside the home say they wouldn't trade their job. They say their job is easier than mine, because you can run in the back room and take a nap. I say, 'What is a nap, what is a nap?' [*laughter*]

SUSAN So what would you like to see happen, Martinique? Do you think women should be given money by the government to stay home, and that would be part of the needed recognition?

MARTINIQUE I don't know if it's a government issue, I don't know. I think a husband should give his wife who's looking after kids a salary at the end of the week. [*laughter*] Not just, 'Here's money for the groceries,' but, 'Here, hon, here is two hundred dollars because I know you worked real hard.' If you don't have a husband, I guess you're just on your own.

SUSAN Yes. Is there a man in your life?

MARTINIQUE Recently I met somebody, and I've been talking to him on the phone—and my oldest girl is having a heart attack. She hasn't met him, and nobody knows anything about it, and I want to keep it that way for now. She was like, 'You have a boyfriend?' And she was like, 'Well, you're not going to see him. You're not going to have time to see him.' I told her, 'Okay, fine, because hey, you go to school all day,' [*laughter*] just like that. He hasn't been here, but she was so upset, and I didn't say his name. She was like, 'What's his name?' She was jealous. I was like, 'Please, I'm not telling you anything. I have to have something that is mine, that you don't have to know about.'

SUSAN That makes sense.

MARTINIQUE So I told her—Monday's her graduation—'I'm going to bring him to the graduation,' and she was having a fit. She said, 'Don't you dare.' I said, 'Well, I'm not coming.' Then she said, 'I want you to come, but I don't want him to come.' So I told her, 'But don't you understand?' She said, 'If you marry him, I'm never calling him "Daddy".' I said, 'I wouldn't want you to. He will not be your father. There is no way I could ever make him be your father.' My mother never made me call her boyfriend 'Dad.' My brother always did, people always thought he was our father. I'm like, That's not my father, are you crazy? I said he would never have that much input in her life. I can't, I can't do that to her.

SUSAN I have one more question. Is there anything I haven't asked you that you'd like to say about mothers and mothering?

MARTINIQUE Being a mother or mothering kids is all what you make it. Some people are not cut out to be mothers. I tell the oldest one—she doesn't know where her mother is, and I don't know if it bothers her, but I tell her—it doesn't really matter, because as long as you have someone who is fulfilling that need, what is the difference? It doesn't have to be your biological parent. We talk a lot about that. None of them want to have natural children, I don't know why. They all want to adopt children. I tell them that's good, as long as you make that child believe from day one that you love him, and so long as you're always honest with that child. When they ask you, 'Are you my real mom?' tell them 'No, but it doesn't matter.' Don't tell them that, 'Oh, I picked you out of a bunch like a cherry.' It doesn't make a difference, you know. If you love children, you love children, that's it.

Raising Fraser

A Special Needs Child

Pat Salter, born in 1952 in Toronto, Ontario
Mother of Fraser
Interviewed by Margaret Dragu

MARGARET When did you decide to have a baby?

PAT When I was over 30, I felt the biological time-clock, and it had something to do with my and Bob's relationship. It was a gesture to solidify our relationship, which had been very on-and-off for so many years.

MARGARET Did you start dreaming about one kind of baby?

PAT There was that undeniable urge that I think lots of women feel around that age—to see something real out there in the world that was part of me and part of Bob, and just to see what we would come up with. It was a very strong urge. The time felt right. I was 31.

MARGARET It happened soon after?

PAT Yes. Exactly after I had got my IUD out. Within five minutes!

MARGARET Were you surprised at what you went through having a baby?

PAT Well, no. I had had a child many years ago as a teenager, so it wasn't my first child. I gave the first one up. I was aware of what was involved with labour and delivery, and my memory of that was not very pleasant, having been 16 years old in the sixties. It was different and not terribly pleasant, so I was prepared for how rough labour can be, and it was a rough labour, but I had information and support and lots of knowledge, and a very understanding doctor. Times had changed around having kids. It wasn't the surgical procedure that it had been in the past—more normal, natural circumstances. Totally different.

MARGARET Do you ever think about that first baby?

PAT I have been just lately trying to do some investigations. Mostly to find out, because Fraser has so many medical, neurological problems, to try to find out if that child had any similar disabilities. It's very difficult to obtain any information from Ontario. Their Adoption Disclosure Act is a lot more open than it is in British Columbia, but there is a very long waiting list of people trying to get information about their adopted children. If I really wanted to pursue this, with medical back-up and doctors pressuring for information and all that kind of thing, I could, but I haven't taken it to that extreme. I have some information on the child up to six months old, which satisfied me that he was unlike Fraser up to six months, that up to then he was pleasant, cheerful, definitely not Fraser.

MARGARET How was Fraser from the time that you came home? I would call Fraser ... a special needs kid. Do you use that term?

PAT Yes, that is the term. I say special needs. Bob tends to use mentally handicapped. I don't particularly feel comfortable with that, so I prefer to use special needs, but Fraser doesn't fit comfortably with a lot of professionals in any particular pigeonhole so, regardless of the fact that I am his parent, he is a difficult child to put any kind of label on. Special needs fits as comfortably as anything else.

MARGARET What are his special needs? Did you notice right away?

PAT I tended to avoid noticing the differences between him and other children. I think it's not uncommon for fathers to pick up on children's disabilities easier than mothers—perhaps because of the emotional closeness, there just seems to be a greater kind of denial that kicks in with the mother. He was about two before we had any professional assessing done with him, but in hindsight, I can remember even before I had been released from St. Paul's having the night nurse come to me and say, 'What is wrong with that kid? He is the only child that is screaming endlessly in the nursery, and he is driving the nursing staff crazy'—at day two or something. At five months old, trying to go work out at South Arm, where you leave your baby to be watched for an hour, they told me they couldn't take him there. I had to quit. So there were indicators. Finally we enrolled him at two-and-a-half in a pre-school, which was typical, but they had some speech-delayed children. At any rate, those teachers finally approached us and asked us if we would have our child assessed. He just wasn't fitting in.

In fact, we were in the process. Bob had gone to the pediatrician and asked him to do a superficial assessment, and that pediatrician had said that, yes, he felt definitely it was necessary to do some further investigation. That's how the ball sort of got rolling. And it was a crusher, because he initially diagnosed him as minimal cerebral dysfunction—they are all just grab-bag terms. This to me was devastating.

MARGARET You were at home a lot with Fraser without being able to have a break. And isolated ...

PAT That always has been part of having a child like Fraser. It is isolating in the sense that, with his particular problems, he doesn't socialize well with other children, so there isn't that night out which a lot of parents have where you just throw a bunch of kids together, and it's a break for you when they play together. He needs to be supervised a lot through the play. Baby-sitting has been a real problem. I work part-time. We have gone through several baby-sitters, and now I still manage to work, but only Bob takes care of him. That is a problem.

MARGARET No one to share your feelings with ... and frightened?

PAT It depends how people react to such a stunning blow. I tend to want to find a plan of action and just move on it, and be busy and do something about it. Knowing where to start was a real battle. There are no manuals out there for mothers. Especially when your child's diagnosis is in kind of a hazy area. He is not Downs, he is not C.P., he's not something very obvious—even to try to explain the way he is to professionals, not having the terminology, for them to get a grasp on what kind of child they are dealing with is difficult. Throughout this whole experience I have been saying, 'I am going to write a manual.' Somebody actually should, but I have learned a great deal about how to do this.

MARGARET What would you suggest to a mom who has a

special needs toddler?

PAT Just recently, I am realizing more and more that the earlier the assessment can be done on the child, the better, and that seems to be the feeling of a lot of professionals that I have encountered. I tended to feel with Fraser that, How can they know what his capabilities are, he is so young? But they can know at 18 months if the child has the potential for behaviour disorders or learning difficulties. They can spot certain signs. I'd recommend early assessment if they have the slightest doubt, if their child is extremely fussy or extremely placid—I wouldn't hesitate to have an assessment done. Just begin with the family doctor. I always have dealt with pediatricians, but a family doctor could certainly do a referral to a pediatrician who could then refer you to a psychologist, and it's all paid for by B.C. Med.

MARGARET What other professionals do you come in contact with?

PAT We've gone to a few. We've been to a gastro-enterologist for Fraser's physical problems. He's been to a series of allergists for his allergies. He's seen neurologists, several psychologists, psychiatrists, occupational therapists, physiotherapists, speech therapists, music therapists. It's a long list. Psychiatrists are not my favourite, allergists are not my favourites either. I have had that very close, open relationship with psychologists, but psychiatrists' approach is just a little more detached, and sometimes I find that quite difficult to deal with. I disagreed in principle with certain allergists, mainly because they tend to push too much in the way of medication, which I really can't agree with for Fraser, because his neurological system is very touchy, and a lot of these drugs set his behaviour off. I have gone with an allergist who has a non-traditional approach, which I have been very happy with, because he doesn't use drugs.

MARGARET Other professionals who have worked with Fraser that you liked?

PAT Definitely music therapists. It is a little bit far outside of what is considered traditional teaching, but what I have seen with Fraser is that a lot of learning can take place that you wouldn't expect to see as far as language development, understanding number concepts, reading concepts, and it's all fun.

MARGARET So he likes it, too. Everybody has to be happy.

PAT Yes.

MARGARET Support group? Finding time for yourself?

PAT We have been involved in several support groups. Some have not been particularly appropriate to Fraser's special needs. Learning Disability Association. We joined their group for a while before we really had a more definitive label. I also encountered a great deal of support through the parents of the preschool he previously attended for a year and a half, and just in passing, having coffee with parents with a variety of needs—and now the school that he is involved with has a parents' group that meets twice weekly, conducted by the social worker. It is quite a structured group, but all of the groups we have been involved with have been tremendously helpful. There's just nothing that can compare with talking to people who really know what you're going through with your child—and also exchanging ideas on how to tackle behaviour problems, different situations—and we have received some very concrete advice from some of the parents in our group that we have been attending since September.

MARGARET Actual example?

PAT Using a timer with trying to get Fraser to dress himself before going to school in the morning. It was a suggestion of one of the other parents, and we've used it. We've only used it on two occasions so far: the idea being that we allow him ample time to dress, but if he isn't dressed when the timer goes off, he has to go to school in what he was wearing when the timer went off, at that point in time. He left one day in a shirt and underpants and socks and nothing else. That has never happened again.

MARGARET What happened at school then?

PAT I cheated. I let him get dressed in the car. It wasn't very comfortable for him—but the nature of the school that he is attending is that they completely go along, they have had children come to school in their pyjamas before. They co-operate completely with the parents.

MARGARET You tell them of the plan.

PAT This was a parent's idea. It was very good, because it isn't Bob, and it isn't me, saying, 'You must get dressed.' It is something outside. I think one of the things I have learned recently—and keep trying to run through my head when I am dealing with Fraser—is that situations such as that are really his problem. I have to stop taking it on, and if I can stand back from the problem, not assume it, then we don't get into the head-to-head battles. In this case the timer is solving it for us.

MARGARET Other examples? Concrete hints?

PAT We're in a bit of a formative stage, as the social worker has had the group take a different direction than it has in previous years, and up to now we have been quite free form and doing a lot of brainstorming, but we have now asked for a little more structure, so we are finding a balance. We have a video or a tape or something specific, and also time for general information exchange.

MARGARET What kind of videos?

PAT We had one video—quite simplistic, but it opened up conversation—that demonstrated bad and good approaches to play with children. For example, taking over unco-operative play with your child. It tried to demonstrate how to catch that balance—to allow the child to take the lead, but not let the play wander off into nothingness. This is also another characteristic of Fraser's particular problem. He does need to be taught how to play. I don't know why that is. His perceptual problems perhaps make it difficult for him. His autistic tendencies to space out—he will lose the direction of the play because his motor skills are affected, it is hard for him to manipulate toys. Sometimes that makes it very frustrating, so we have to re-learn how to approach play in order to help him. Play is essential for everyone, particularly for children.

MARGARET Having children helps you rediscover play. How do you balance remaining a person by yourself, as well as remaining a mother?

PAT I don't think anyone can really be prepared for how much parenting does change their life. I had enough friends around with children that I got some idea. I didn't go into it completely blind. But we led a pretty self-centred, pleasure-seeking life, doing whatever we chose to do—so it was a shock. The most difficult thing was having to employ so much structure in your day-to-day life. We were quite unstructured. Just providing for a child, you do have to maintain somewhat of a schedule—and then, Fraser with his autistic tendency does thrive on tighter structured scheduling, which almost makes me—I can't stand the idea of it, but it really is best for him, so we really had to pull up our socks in that regard. We are far from ideal, but we try.

Having to deal with all the things I had to deal with with Fraser has taken its toll on our, mine and Bob's, relationship, definitely, I think because I have been placed under so much stress. Normally Bob takes on the stress in the family, and he seems to enjoy it, and I have always been the more laid-back one in the relationship, but it's no longer the case.

My level of stress is now very high, so what we have done is, we have discovered respite care. It's provided by the Ministry of Housing and Social Services. It varies from municipality to municipality. Here in Richmond, we have one house which will take children for blocks of 24 hours, special needs kids. It's run by the Richmond Society for Special People, and there is a minimal charge, basically no charge, as long as they feel you and your child qualify for respite. We qualify. Knowing all that and talking to other parents who used this care, it still took us, it was quite a leap for us to take Fraser there for the first 24-hour time, but we are getting to like it. We don't use the maximum number of blocks of hours we can use—I forget the total number you can use—we are nowhere near approaching our limit on it. It seems to be working out at once every two months, we will take him for a 24- or 48-hour period.

MARGARET What do you do during this time?

PAT Well, we went away twice this summer when he was in care, and it was just wonderful. The first time we went away, to Orcas Island, it was a surprise to us to find how much we enjoyed each other's company again, and how much we laughed. We laughed our heads off all the time we were away.

It was just ... incredible relief ... just to have that stress away for a short period of time. The setting, the staff, are wonderful. The setting is not ideal, there is a lot going on, and other municipalities offer the same kind of care in a family home. This is more of an institutional setting, which some people don't particularly agree with, and the children who go there seem to be quite physically disabled, so it doesn't offer a challenge for Fraser. It would probably be more beneficial for him to be with more typical children, for him to model after, but we are still happy with it. He likes to go there. There is one particular staff member whom he really likes. Every time he has gone, he has gotten sick though, homesickness. He gets physically sick, he starts vomiting. I feel a twinge of guilt when I get him back when he is sick, but I think the positive benefits really outweigh anything else—and it's for everyone. I find I have so much more patience with him when he gets back.

MARGARET Anything else for stress?

PAT Exercise is good. There isn't much.

MARGARET Any other recommendations to a person with a special needs kid?

PAT If there is any possible way, don't do it alone. Spread out the responsibility, the care of your child. Just milk every possible resource, family and otherwise. Don't be afraid to do it. You are only taxing yourself and not doing your child any good whatsoever by taking it all on. Also, don't be afraid to second-guess doctors. There are plenty of organizations you can call if you have questions about any kind of medication or treatment.

MARGARET Any particular books?

PAT I have quite a number of books. *The Impossible Child*. There are plenty of them. And keep phoning.

The Male Child

Is He Different?

Jane Grant, born in 1952 in rural Ontario
Mother of Peter
Interviewed by Diane Martin

DIANE Okay, Jane, give us some background.

JANE I'm 39. My son's name is Peter, and he's seven. I'm married and have been for 12 years. My husband's name is Matt. I'm a counsellor, a consultant, and a student. I was a Public Health nurse for 10 years before I went back to school to get a Master's degree in counselling.

DIANE What kind of counselling do you do?

JANE Long-term therapy. I help people deal with traumas, problems from their childhood, or relationship problems they are having that probably came about from something in their background, and I have some extra training in sexual abuse and working with dysfunctional families, such as the families of alcoholics.

DIANE Your clients are mostly female. Do you think that's because you are female, or is it because most people who seek therapy are female?

JANE It's some of both. More women come to therapy than men, because it's more socially acceptable for them to seek something outside and to express it, but more men are starting to come as they are recognizing their own pain and are not feeling as silenced. I don't think women are coming to therapy because they are more sick than men.

DIANE At what point did you think, 'I would like to get pregnant'?

JANE In my twenties, I started to feel that sense of longing. I wasn't involved with anybody, and I started thinking about how I could accommodate this need or feeling of wanting a baby, without a long-term relationship. I knew of women who were doing that kind of thing. They were in lesbian relationships. I didn't have the same kind of social network available to me, so I didn't know how I was going to accommodate that need.

DIANE You were aware that a social network was necessary, though?

JANE Oh yes, absolutely. I never felt that I could or would want to have a child in isolation. To do something isolating in an isolating context would be impossible.

DIANE It's interesting that you had enough awareness to see that. A lot of women—when they get pregnant, they really don't have a sense of the kind of isolation they're going to face until they are actually in it.

JANE I had a sense of isolation in advance, but I still wasn't prepared for it. We lived in the house where we are now. It's on a street that has a park at the end, it has several community centres, it has lots of neighbours, but not that many neighbours that stay home. I hadn't got to know my community, and I didn't feel part of it other than as a professional who was coming home. I didn't know a lot of people. I remember one day in February or March—Peter was born in January—I had him inside a big furry coat and I was walking the streets trying to find a mobile unit that was a drop-in centre just north and east of us—I couldn't find it and I was just desperate.

DIANE You were looking for a parent-child drop-in.

JANE Yes. I'd phoned and asked about it. Here I was, a Public Health nurse for seven or eight or nine years by then, having been an advocate for people, knowing how to access community resources, and I couldn't even find our local drop-in centre. I just felt so silenced. I felt so out of my element. I was scared of Peter. He was tense. I was tense. He had colic. I felt he robbed me of a lot of my skills. It was scary, and being in a depression, too, you don't function the way you do for somebody else.

Matt and I have always had a partnership, and we have it again now, but during that time, I was at home in the track pants, and he was going to work, and much as we'd talked about it and tried not to get into this, he would come home at the end of the day, and things would be messy, and he would say, 'What have you done all day?' I'd be ready to deck him, and I'd been scrambling all day feeling desperate. There'd be periods of time during which I'd forget to open the curtains, so that the days and the nights would sort of blur in together.

DIANE It's not healthy to be alone with a baby that much. Let's talk about your family. How did your mother feel when Peter was born?

JANE Oh, she was really pleased. She was really happy. Now, I don't think this has ever been explicitly said, but boys have a special place in our family. I suspect they are extra-valued because they are seen as an essential resource, that they would take care of us financially, that they were more responsible, that they were out in the world in a way that we, as women, were not. Their role as providers was idealized, but I think both roles are an illusion. My mother's role as emotional caretaker was an illusion, too.

DIANE You have one brother?

JANE Yes, who is five years older. That's certainly the way I felt in my family. Although I think I was in some respects more valued by my father.

DIANE Because you were the baby girl?

JANE Yes, and he and I had some kind of relationship for much longer than my brother and my dad did. We enjoyed each other more. I don't know whether it was because they just didn't hit it off, or because my brother already had a relationship with my mother established when I was born.

DIANE When Peter was born, did you have some sense that his gender was being celebrated as much as his birth?

JANE In a hidden way. Certainly I never wanted to talk about it. My brother had had a marriage and it didn't last. Then he was in another marriage and didn't have any children—I had the child first. I had the boy child. I'd had a first pregnancy that didn't carry, and through this next pregnancy, till almost seven months, Matt and I assumed it would be a girl.

DIANE But you didn't know before he was born?

JANE No, but our doctor started making some comments about the way I was carrying.

DIANE That it would be a girl?

JANE No, he wondered if it would be a boy. When a couple of other people made those comments, we thought, well, we'd better start [*laughs*] thinking about this possibility. I find it an interesting sort of contradiction.

DIANE Why did you both want a girl?

JANE I had certain issues with boys and men. I had an idealized image of men that would crash down when I could allow myself to see them as real and not magical beings who were stronger than me and could do everything. I can confront and risk conflict with men more easily than with women, and I have come to a clearer place about what is reasonable to expect of a man—I mean honesty, the ability to take emotional risks, and staying power, to name a few things. Still, at some deep core place, I felt more connected to women, and I wasn't sure I would know how to talk to a male child. I was scared to death of what a male child would do when it grew up.

DIANE Can you explain this more?

JANE I really hate the notion of women as victims. Women collude in making the power structures of our society, and women can be perpetrators of violence in the home. My experience as a therapist has shown me that women have violent feelings that bubble up—they beat their kids, they sexually abuse their children. But it is still a culture where men are valued more than women, and I didn't want raising a son to help perpetuate the overt economic power men hold over women in our society. You know, as soon as women have children, we lose our financial independence.

DIANE How did Matt feel about having a baby?

JANE Matt also really wanted a girl child. He's a nurse. He spends most of his life relating to women. He had an older sister and a mother. His dad died when he was eight, and his brother is younger, so he has more of a woman-oriented view.

DIANE What happened when the doctor said, 'It's a boy'?

JANE The doctor said, 'It's a boy,' and Pete peed on the doctor's foot—he loves hearing that story. Matt and I both burst into tears, and I just felt this huge swell of love for him—it was a ... I was going to say bizarre experience—and thank god, or the goddess or whoever, that it happened, because I would've hated to have a male child and then not bond to it. Ever since then, we see Peter first and his gender second. Peter is our baby. He's our boy. He's our child. The issues around his gender are something we're working on in terms of the issues in society around male privilege, power, and violence, as well as the taboo against men being able to verbalize and nurture and cuddle. He wasn't a cuddly baby, so I used to wonder about that. Some babies are born irritable. Couple that with a mother who was so tense and so scared—we weren't a good baby-mother combination, but he was massaged and touched a lot. I sang to him a lot. Because of his irritability and colic and stiffness he was carried *a lot*.

Now he loves to be caressed and stroked. He loves it when I sing to him. He sits on our laps. He gives hugs. People talk about how boys aren't touched as much as girls. I don't think that's his case. When it's your child, it's your child, it doesn't matter what the gender is.

Matt and I collaborate as to what are the best ways to look after Peter. Our gender comes into it. I can talk about the time Peter was inside me, and Matt can't. He and Peter can giggle about how their penises tickle when they go over a bump in the road, and I don't know what they're talking about. We have these differences which we can celebrate, but they don't control our attitude to child-raising.

DIANE Are you and Peter very close?

JANE There's a poem by Bronwen Wallace, called 'Melons at the Speed of Light,' that triggered something for me. She's writing about her son who is turning 10 that summer. 'Every morning, he plays baseball in the park next door, / leaving me quiet for coffee and the paper. / But it never works. It's his voice, rising / through the noise of the game, that shapes me still, / the way, years earlier, his turning knotted my belly, / the kick under the ribs, aimed at the heart.' Then she talks a bit more about how she has to go over and watch him play ball. She's going through this process about how she's the one who needs to grow up. She writes, 'this is what my son knows already; he just wants to get on with it.' That last sentence—'he just wants to get on with it'—

sat with me for a long time. I had strong negative reactions, and yet I think it's very real, this poem.

I realized that a lot of literature is silent on mother/son stuff, especially radical feminist literature that advocates separating the raising of boys and girls. They seem to say, 'Why are we wasting energy on boy children anyway?' I don't agree with that position. Another position advocates raising boys in a more feminist-oriented society, to hope they'll grow up and there'll be a difference. I'm not sure about this one, either.

DIANE That it's our responsibility, as mothers, to raise men so they don't turn into Marc Lépines?

JANE That's still going to leave it all up to the mothers. It's not our sole responsibility to raise non-violent boys. Mothers are *one* person in their children's lives. I'm not going to be responsible for a violent action he makes. That is his responsibility. The reality is that both women and men *have* to be different in themselves, before change is going to happen. So where does that start?

DIANE Where everything else starts. With the mother. [*laughs*]

JANE That's the expectation. But what we're trying to do in our little unit is broaden that. So it includes Matt, it includes Peter. Peter at seven has to be responsible for his behaviour. If he gets angry, he can't blame it on Matt or me. He's responsible. This poem, that line 'he just wants to get on with it,' really upset me, because I knew unconsciously that's exactly the battle I'd been struggling with for several years—this sense of what happens in our society, that mothers get thrown out with the wash as boys grow into men and go into the real world. Or that mothers are supposed to let them go. That causes me great pain, thinking about doing that with my son. Because he's—

DIANE He's your baby.

JANE That's right, and I'm his mom.

DIANE Yes, and it's okay for a girl to be tied to her mother's apron strings—you don't even hear this expression in reference to girls, but you hear it in a negative way about boys being tied to their mothers. You hear about the domineering mother. The consuming mother.

JANE And where is the reality of just a really rich, warm relationship, where there's interconnection and mutual affection and interdependence and caring, along with each person having a sense of themselves? That's what I've been coming to—learning how to be that for myself and in my relationship with Matt and Peter, and trying to teach him that too. Knowing that we're dealing with a very powerful society out there that really encourages anything but what we're trying to develop. All I can do is hope that he'll live a life that in some way incorporates that. If he doesn't, then I'll have to learn how to accept that. My goal is to offer a process that doesn't make this rupture necessary. It's hard work.

DIANE Would you describe a day in your life—what it's like for the mother of a seven year old? A day in the life of you. Right now, you do have two occupations outside the house as well as being a mother. You're a therapist and you're taking a Master's degree in education.

JANE Yes, right now it's really intense because I'm writing my Master's thesis on motherhood as an institution versus the reality; it's titled, 'An Exploration of Awareness and Its Place in Dealing With the Dilemmas of Motherhood.' The paper is an outcome of what Matt and Pete and I have negotiated. I'm spending a lot of time away from the family right now because of it. For example, yesterday, I worked in the evening and got home in time to be with Matt and Peter while they were watching the All-Star game. They had had popcorn, and they made some more for me so I could have some. They'd pulled out the living-room couch bed, and they were on it. When I got home, Pete wanted me to tickle his back as we watched the game. Matt was in and out. In between innings, Pete and I talked about his day to sort of catch up, and I told Pete a bit about my day.

This morning I didn't see Pete—which is atypical—because he slept in. Normally we have breakfast and chat about the plans for the day. Fight about what chores he's supposed to get done. [*laughs*] Then I worked on my thesis, and made phone calls to find some books and locate some things, and to some of my clients. It was supervision day, so in the afternoon there were two hours of supervision with three of my peers. Then I did some more research for my paper and went home. On the way, I stopped to see Pete playing ball hockey, and I chatted with Matt. We were planning a family evening. For a while we hadn't felt Pete was old enough for this film, but he saw Kevin Costner in *Robin Hood*—that was a mixed reaction, all this *ooooh* real violence—but he liked Costner, so we thought we'd try *Field of Dreams*. He really liked it. Then we went for a walk, and we talked some more about his day and what was going to happen for the rest of the week. We negotiated how many times he could go to the store and how much money he could have to go to the store—he can't go to the store every day.

DIANE Sounds like a rather nice day, actually.

JANE It was. It was a really nice day, and it was planned that way. Now today, in contrast, I have a meeting with my therapist, a meeting with my faculty advisor, and one with a client who is in crisis, as well as some chart writing, and another client before I go home and plan with Matt how we're dealing with Peter for the next two weeks.

DIANE Because the summer holidays are upon us.

JANE And figuring out how the child is going to be covered. This is the first year that Matt has participated in organizing all of that, and we had a debate about what I was going to do. Pete decided he didn't want to do anything structured, not even swimming lessons, so this year he's going to camp a couple of times, and Matt is taking three weeks' holiday throughout the summer, and he's taking responsibility for Pete during those times, and he knows a couple of people he can call if he needs some time off. And I feel guilty, but not that guilty! [*laughs*] We're sharing this kind of thing a lot more. You know, when I started telling you about this, I started feeling guilty, because I know that many of the other women being interviewed will have talked about a really difficult day, where the burden is mainly on them. I feel guilty because I'm not in that place. But I wouldn't trade places—

DIANE It's a no-win situation, isn't it?

JANE Absolutely.

DIANE And all those women feel guilty as well. Or have, I think. All women feel guilty no matter what's happening—the guilt of having someone else with your child, even if it's your partner.

JANE Yes—*I* should be doing this, *I* shouldn't be taking this summer to work on this research paper—but I have to have this research paper done—I shouldn't be burdening Matt—oh god.

DIANE How did being a mother change your image of yourself?

JANE I've been in therapy for three-and-a-half years, and I had a short-term course of counselling before Peter's birth and went back to the counsellor for a short period after his birth to deal with the absolute panic and depression. I've been learning how to parent myself, so that I can parent him—I believe if I don't know how to take care of myself, I can't possibly do a reasonable job of taking care of him. I see that as a responsibility and an obligation, but I also see it as a really wonderful thing to do for myself.

DIANE It sounds like motherhood sharpened your sense of self. You had an identity as a professional before Peter was born, but perhaps afterwards you had greater respect for what that meant to you.

JANE Well, I had some sense of myself. Absolutely. The crisis that came was the de-selfing.

DIANE De-selfing?

JANE When I had Pete. Giving to someone else. Living through someone else. Not paying attention to what my needs are. That's what motherhood does.

DIANE How long did it take you to get your sense of self back?

JANE I went back to work when he was nine months old, but I wasn't really on the road to where I am until he was three or four.

DIANE How did motherhood affect you as a feminist?

JANE I wasn't what I understood to be a feminist until after Pete was born. For a long time I lived a feminist way of being, but I didn't start reading the literature or aligning myself with the feminist community until the early eighties. I went to a conference, Don't Blame Mother, in '85, on women in therapy.

Paula Caplan was one of the keynote speakers. Judith Arcana was there, Phyllis Chesler was there. This was when Peter was around two years old.

Have you read any of Carol Gilligan's work? She's a developmental psychologist who has done a lot of work on women's development being different from men's. She's recently written a book called *Making Connections*, talking about how girls in their socialization go underground at a certain point, just pre-adolescence. Their self is hidden inside, but they're resistors. I think that's what I was. When I was pre-Peter and early Peter—that was becoming more vocal. Certainly, even in the early eighties, I wasn't reading a lot of feminist literature. First of all, I didn't know about it, which now just amazes me.

I've lived in Toronto since I went to university. I lived in New College, and there's a women's studies library there—it's been there for years. I started using it this year! Motherhood has been a spring-board to a lot of things, in a more public way. I've been fighting and resisting in my relationship with Matt since I met him, and I've done a lot of mainstream stuff like going into nursing and what have you, and being a good girl, but, yes, motherhood really brought the politicization.

DIANE What are your biggest problems now, in terms of being a mother?

JANE As I grow in my sense of who I want to be and who I am as Pete's mom, that's caused several mini-crises in my relationship with Matt, which has required him to either keep up or get out—or for me to negotiate it with him or me get out. Sometimes we've talked, and sometimes we've ridden it out. There've been a lot of choice-points, about whether or not we were both going to be able to do it together. That's bigger than motherhood, but certainly the motherhood issue has been one of the locations where we've fought it out. I see that that is going to be a problem as long as we live together—because of how we're socialized. But so far, we keep working on it, negotiating and figuring out what we want as individuals and together, and what we want for Pete.

For example, we have problems around his baseball right now.

We have that around his hockey in the winter. Peteua's a very sports-inclined kid, and those sports are really part of our social structure that stinks. Hockey more so. Baseball to me, I don't know if it's my bias because Matt has indoctrinated me, but baseball to me has something else that goes with it. I don't know what it is—the structure of the baseball leagues is very much a part of the patriarchal society—but I don't see the same kind of aggression in it that I see in hockey.

DIANE Nobody talks about baseball parents the way they talk about hockey parents.

JANE But they're there! It's a more sophisticated kind of aggression that the parents get into in little league. Pete's league is in a community that people would label blue collar, and there are a lot of different kinds of mixes of parents there—but they all seem to want their team to go out there and get that other team. A big concern is how we're all going to live with Peter's sports abilities and incorporate that into the lifestyle and philosophy that we're working on. Right now he's talking about a sports career, and who knows, at 21, where that would be? I hope that's not where he ends up, but I hope I can live with it and be a reasonable, supportive parent if that's what he chooses.

The other biggest problem—it was *the* big problem for most of the past year—was around school. School came alive to me as another unsafe place. It brought back a lot of memories of my own childhood, and I don't think it has changed that much since when I was a kid. It's just more slick. Interestingly, Matt got as distraught about it as I did—about how Pete was being taught, the violence we hear about in the school yard, the attitude of the principal, the tone of voice we would hear adults speaking to children in. It wasn't bothering Pete that much, according to him. But when he talks about his new school, he says he really can't wait.

DIANE What's the difference between the new school and the old school?

JANE The new school's a house. The families are fairly actively involved. The people who own it used it as a way to get their own children through the system. They deal with gender issues, they deal with power issues, there's negotiation of relationships and conflicts and differences. There's an awareness of the bigger social context, bigger than what is in front of your nose. There are creative ways of learning. It strikes me that we don't really have reasonable expectations of children. Somebody commented to me recently how everyone gets so excited when a four-year-old ties his shoe-laces. If we remember back to the good old days in farming communities, girls and boys at three and four would be looking after younger siblings, helping with meal preparation, and some of the girls were being taught needlework at that age. We get really excited if a kid makes a gesture toward doing up a shoe-lace.

DIANE We get out the video camera! It's true, we get excited over every little thing, which perhaps isn't preparing children very well for—

JANE Reality! And also play, there's something about play—and toys and play—I'm not sold on any more at all. I've never liked it.

DIANE Never liked what?

JANE Play. Like Lego and imaginative toy figures. I couldn't relate to it.

DIANE When you were a kid?

JANE No, now. With Peter. It's another way we keeps kids segregated. We keep them in an artificial, unreal world. Some toys are great, but the average kid's experience today is, you walk into the room, and it's wall-to-wall toys. It's not representative of the real world, and Pete doesn't play with them much. I don't mean that children shouldn't play. They should play every minute of their lives. It's what they're playing, how they're playing it, what they're being told to play with, how it's constructed, and where it's supposed to be done. It's supposed to be done in this nice little private home, away from the real world.

DIANE Even out of the living room and the kitchen.

JANE Oh, absolutely—it removes them even more from reality, and that's a problem I'm having more and more. I don't want my kid removed from reality. On the one hand, this school looks like it's out of reality. On the other, a lot of the stuff that they do is very much about contemporary reality. It's a dilemma.

DIANE Let's talk specifically about what you see the school system perpetuating, particularly with Peter. What exactly are you reacting to? When Peter came home from school and told you things, what was it that made you say, 'Let's look at a private school for him for next year.'

JANE It wouldn't be just what he'd come home and say. It would be when I would go to school to do activities and what I would see. Subtle things like having a party—and I feel like I'm building mountains out of molehills—and the girls are at one table and the boys are at the other. Under the girls' table it's a bit messy, under the boys' table it's messy. The teacher yelled at the girls for being messy. Not a word was said to the boys. More was said to the girls around aggressive behaviour than to the boys, as if it was a given and accepted.

The school system duplicates the structure of the home. The principal, whether male or female, is the power figure, and it depends on that person, whether the structure either flies or it flops. It is not a community network where everybody is coming together for the good of the group and negotiating what the group needs. Certainly the people who own the school take a lot of the leadership and responsibility for the maintenance of it and the overall responsibility for the quality of the program, but in the day-to-day experience, it's very collegial right down to the youngest kid. In the regular system, kids are compartmentalized in the classroom, and you see that duplicated on the playground. It's not socially okay for a grade three and a grade one to play much together.

DIANE What else?

JANE It was also what we heard about violence in the school yard. Either physical violence and children getting hurt, or sexualized violence. Two boys were ganging up on one of the girls Peter liked in his class, and chasing her around at recesses, and trying to grab her so that they could hug and kiss her, and I don't know what else. Pete wouldn't talk about that. Some of the other kids tried to help her get away from that.

DIANE I watched it one day when I was in the school yard with Emma, and I could hardly stand it.

JANE Pete went through a period where he didn't like what he was seeing, and he said that he and another boy would try at times to get the boys to stop it and help her out. Then that all went underground. We didn't hear anything about it for quite a while. Then, later this spring, Pete had talked about his teacher saying that if things didn't settle down, the children were going to have to start writing notes to their parents to talk about things they had been reprimanded for at school. Apology things. Two days later, Pete brought a note home, and we got a phone call from his teacher. We were both really confused and distraught about it. It turned out Pete was one of the boys who grabbed this same girl's privates. We just didn't know what to make of it. We still don't. We think he made a bad choice. We asked him how that fit with how he'd been with this girl before. He'd also talked about how one of the boys went around grabbing another boy's crotch and using the expression 'suck my cock.' Well, Peter didn't like it and wouldn't want them to do it to him. He didn't participate, and yet he did somewhat the same thing with this girl, and I think it confused him, and I think he made a bad decision, and we've talked about it. He has to learn from bad decisions.

DIANE If Peter doesn't meet your expectations, how do you deal with that?

JANE We start by talking about it, and we talk about how we have a right to these expectations. It varies how it's dealt with. If we have to speak to him more than once about something we know is a reasonable expectation, we either do it with him right at that moment, or, if it's not something that needs to be done urgently, if he's giving us a hard time, we'll send him to his room. It really varies.

DIANE Depending on what has happened?

JANE And on the intensity of his reaction, and what's going on in the bigger context. There are times when we could put an expectation on him to do what he's supposed to do when we realize that he's really in a state, and if we stay with being rigid on that, that's not being reasonable, and we need to give him an opportunity to cool down, or us an opportunity to cool down. If some kind of scene's happened between him and me, fairly shortly after that I'll try to see if he's willing to talk about it, and I'll apologize for my part in it. It's usually my part, there is my part in it, and he's learning to apologize for his part in it. We'll talk about what that was.

Where I have my biggest problem when I'm disciplining is, I over-talk with him, and I over-analyze with him. Matt and I are getting better at helping each other sift and sort when we're clicking into whatever our unhelpful mode is. We're also learning how to say, 'We're not perfect, we make mistakes, and you're just going to have to live with that.' We try not to hit him. There are times when we feel we've made violent gestures. When I raise my voice and get really angry, and Matt, too, we feel that's violent, and we're not happy with that. We can't get rid of everything.

DIANE No, you're human. But as a rule, talking and removing him from your company is what you do?

JANE That's one of the ways. Or I'll leave the room. It's separating ourselves somehow. If we stay together, we're either going to start bugging him and nagging him or get violent in our language or yelling or out of control, and none of us wants to do that, so it's to give us all a time out in some way—but one of us leaves.

DIANE What about consequences?

JANE Sometimes we'll ask him, when certain kinds of things happen, what he thinks a reasonable consequence is, and when it happens, we say, 'Remember what you said? Well, that's what's happening.' He doesn't like that! [*laughs*] That we take him at his word.

DIANE He catches himself in his own snare.

JANE Well, it makes him a bit more accountable.

DIANE That the consequences for certain kinds of behaviour follow logically from what the behaviour was, and that Pete sees the logic.

JANE Yes.

DIANE Is there anything else that you'd like to say?

JANE I'd like to add something about Peter as a boy child. I'm not sure how different it is from a girl child, but I know in our society, it's perceived as different. I think that's because there's an expectation that what we're raising these children to be is very, very different. As we try to get away from that as a goal, we come more and more to understand what each of us needs to do as people, but we're always in this double experience. We also know there's the outside world to face, and I can't help wondering how my world at home and the outside world are going to meet. We're supposed to be preparing him for that external world. How are those two going to meet?

The One O'Clock Club

Motherhood In a London Slum

Morgan Goodchild, born in 1939 in London, England
Mother of one daughter and two sons
Interviewed by Margaret Dragu

MORGAN I used to go around by myself when my sister was at school, playing games with my dolls and calling myself 'Gently.' That was the name I chose for myself.

MARGARET How old were you?

MORGAN Around four.

MARGARET That's a lovely name.

MORGAN Isn't it wonderful? It belongs to that era, and fairy-tales and those stories about Rose Red and Snow White.

MARGARET When did you first want to have a baby?

MORGAN I never wanted to have a baby before I had a baby. I didn't think about having a baby until after I'd had an abortion, and I got pregnant quite soon afterwards—about a year, which was very common in those days, before the Pill. It wasn't until I actually had my daughter that I felt ecstatic and involved and became anxious and did nothing else, absolutely nothing else for that period.

MARGARET Were you surprised by this change after you had the baby? That you became a different person with different concerns?

MORGAN Well, I was young—18 when I was pregnant, and 19 when I had her. It was a time of change, leaving home, leaving school, and not really knowing what I was up to. It just seemed natural, because lots of people did have babies before the Pill. It was something you tried to avoid if you were sexually active. Pregnancy seemed to be a stage in your life. When I first started to menstruate, I hated it. It wasn't something I had looked forward to. I thought, Damn! That's how I felt when I got pregnant. Yet when I had the baby, suddenly there was another person there, not a condition, not any more a stage in my life, it was a stage in her life. So it was a kind of, what shall we say?

MARGARET A flowering?

MORGAN Well, a separation, a duplicating, and—

MARGARET Replicating?

MORGAN Yes, replicating, and I went on with my life, with her being central to it. What shook me was, she needed so much protection, and I felt terribly irresponsible and uninformed and frightened about just keeping her alive. Like when you are a kid and you have tortoises and gerbils and something happens to them. You think, Oh god, something better not happen to this one! What's wrong with it? Why is it crying? You feel very sort of untutored. You are thrown into this life-and-death situation.

MARGARET And you were surprised by that?

MORGAN Not surprised, I was shocked by it. In fact, I don't think people noticed it in me. I used to notice with other people, which was why I didn't want to get pregnant at the time. It was all just laundry, and you couldn't go out when you wanted to, or without taking a lot of stuff with you and being back at a certain time. Suddenly you were terribly burdened. You were very rarely walking around outside your house without carrying something. That's what I noticed very much in other people, and suddenly it came upon me.

I used to project her into the future, which gives me a funny feeling, now that she is 30. I feel as if I'm living through having children. It's a sort of funny vertiginous feeling of living in my own past and my own present and my own future. Before, I used to wonder, what was she going to be like when she was four, no longer lying on her back wrapped up in woolly things? What was she going to be like walking about with no diapers, like a little girl? It's the same now that she is 30. I think of this baby that I used to carry about—and I think of particular photographs—I somehow feel that I have stepped into my future. I'm not sure if I'm 19 or 50. It has gotten confused. It's a nice feeling and something to do with a life's cycle that you are responsible for, in the framework of your own life. Do you ever have that?

MARGARET Sort of a simultaneous time feeling?

MORGAN It's never happened to me except with my children.

I suppose because the three-year-old is still very much there in the 30-year-old. It puts me in contact with my own clear memories of being very little.

MARGARET Yes, I found after having Aretha that my whole sense of self, and my mother and my childhood, my mother's childhood and the whole framework of my family, primarily the girl children—I could remember things from my childhood that were unleashed like a Pandora's box. That's what I am relating to when you say you were shocked by some of the feelings you had at home—not just wandering around with perambulators, but the inside life, where you were so responsible and so frightened, and you were shocked to find that. I wonder, why is it such a secret? Did your mother ever talk to you about being a mother?

MORGAN No, I had my first child when I was 19, and my mother got married when she was 19, but she didn't have my older sister until she was 24, which seemed to me quite a long time to wait in those days. I don't think she was that keen on children, really. It didn't seem to be part of my parents' immediate need or desire, to make a family. You often see in a Chinese community that women will have their babies and the grandmother looks after them. I don't think it is natural to be left absolutely alone to look after a baby.

MARGARET One woman all by herself?

MORGAN One woman all by herself, not even one woman with a husband. I think it is good in lots of ways of course, but I think it puts too much responsibility on you. I don't have any younger brothers and sisters. I don't remember my mother going through any of these traumas. I think it probably would have been quite concealed. She would have gone off to hospital and returned with a baby, and I wouldn't have known anything about it. With my own children, I had my third child by accident by myself at home. My daughter was there—she wasn't there immediately for the delivery, but she had to make herself busy and sort of keep out of the way while I had a baby—and there was a lot of excitement.

MARGARET How old was she?

MORGAN She was nine. She was very excited, and I feel that she was lucky. I was taken away to hospital and kept there unnecessarily because of bureaucracy—I had signed in. Because I hadn't had attention during the delivery, they wanted to observe the baby—and he wasn't all right after all. He had a lung infection, which I believe was due to being put in an ambulance and dragged about. I think we would have been better off if we had been left where we were.

MARGARET So your daughter had an experience similar to that of of rural life.

MORGAN I was living in a terrible slum when this happened, in a block of flats in London—on the ground floor. People parked their cars right outside in the courtyard. The neighbours knew I was pregnant. I realized I had to go to hospital, and then I realized it was too late. I was all sort of packed and ready to go, and I had to get unpacked and get back into bed and have this baby. We didn't have a phone. It was really bad. So my husband rushed off, not realizing how imminent it was, to find a phone, which was impossible in South London at the time. They were all wrenched out by the entrails for a huge radius. They were vandalized. It was the practice to tear telephones out by their roots. He was out looking for a phone—not to phone an ambulance, but to tell the hospital he was bringing me in by car. The neighbours saw all this activity and figured out I was having a baby. A huge crowd of people gathered, like I was the Queen, outside my door. I could hear them talking: 'Has she had it yet?' It was so funny. I took no notice of them. They had to be driven away from the door when the ambulance came.

I had little fits of feeling very angry, and then I'd think that it was great, because lots of people would never really talk to me. I did see them afterwards. They all came to the door and told me about their confinements, and if I wasn't there, they told my husband—he heard a lot about their labours and their problems. I became a part of the community in a different way. I discovered lesbian relationships among these working-class housewives. Passionate relationships amongst these really tough women. They would be out playing football sometimes—just mothers from rough families with tough husbands. They had relationships where they would sort of fall out and cry and not speak to each other and then make up and then—I got into all of this. Up until then they were a bit suspicious of me. We were a bit out of place, and they wondered what we were doing. We were artists.

MARGARET It's enormously equalizing, isn't it? Having a baby. You do have something in common with people you wouldn't say *boo* to in the bank line-up.

MORGAN It's true. I would go to the park. They had what they called the One O'Clock Club, a sort of play centre for kids, very much a social club for working-class mothers who went there every day from one o'clock, after lunch, until picking up other children from school, about four. There was a hut and, come rain or come shine, we would go into this hut and there was such community—and the people, I would never have met those people in any other way, these women were not women I would socialize with.

Sometimes I would have tea with them, or sometimes they would take my children to their house for tea, or I would take their children home to my place. That was the basis of our socializing. We didn't extend it beyond that or arrange to go out together. We didn't expect to have any more than that in common. There was sort of a curiosity sometimes, about how we lived. I really missed that when I first came to Vancouver. My children were still small, and I felt terribly isolated.

MARGARET You didn't get to know each others' husbands?

MORGAN No, it was a completely separate world that went on during the day. They would go home and make their husbands' meals. Several of the women I know worked in the local school, which I thought was very good. Kids in England have school dinners, hot dinners, cooked dinners in the middle of the day, which are subsidized, depending on your means, so that employed a whole lot of these women, cooking and serving meals. They had playground supervisors. There was much more supervision, especially in London, because of heavy road traffic, and kids were not allowed out once they were in there playing.

But they were not supervised by teachers. They were supervised by people who were employed. Not volunteers either, just local mothers. In the classes, they would have an assistant, too, to pick things up and wipe things up, take kids to the lavatory.

MARGARET Did you do any part-time jobs like that? Were you working at this point?

MORGAN No, I didn't. My time was terribly full. A lot of women didn't. I had a lot of friends who were in my situation, who were artists of some kind, not practising as artists because they had children. They didn't expect to. This was part of life. It would come to an end, and then they would resume somehow. There wasn't a great deal of pressure to keep things going.

MARGARET They didn't feel pressured to keep producing art?

MORGAN Well, they weren't successful economically, so they weren't losing money through not being artists. These women, because they had their children younger, prior to the Pill, had either been to art school and left to have babies, or had just finished art school and then had a baby, so they didn't have that feeling of losing money or status. They were much more satisfied creatively just looking after their children.

I think we had a much better social life in our roles as mothers of young children. It wasn't anything you had to work into your social life, it developed your social life. I found it endlessly interesting. I was very conscious that this was a time in my life I would never retrieve, and it was very short. It had to do with my young womanhood and my children's childhood. I could find a way of earning money and pursue art—I was doing illustration at the time. I couldn't live this part of my life later, because it was too ephemeral. It isn't forever. You have terrible nights without sleeping, when you feel like a rag, true, but you recover.

I think that for women who are professional in some way, the professional world is very questionable, but having a baby is not questionable at all. There are a lot of questions about it. I think, Forget it, stop talking about it. If you have a baby and you stay at home and look after it for those two or three years, you don't have to argue. You don't have to defend it. I think you're gaining far more than you lose by the experience. You can take it even further. You can really build a career at any time in your life. I believe that you can. You find something that you are good at, that you like, that will bring you money. That is what I call a career. You can do that at certain times in your life more easily than others, but you will never again have that time of your life when you are a young woman having children.

My three-year-old is now 30. The baby I accidentally had by myself is now 19. I have three children, two boys and a girl. They are all friends of mine now. A baby's life has a time limit. That's one of the things that's very hard about handing your children over to the school system, because it's not necessarily a system that you agree with. It's very hard trying to find the right school. In England I was lucky, and in Canada I was not.

MARGARET You're handing them over to a whole bureaucracy and political system, and they have them for hours and hours each day.

MORGAN Sometimes you say things off the top of your head. A friend of mine told me her child's teacher—it was summer, and the child had little leather sandals on, and the teacher sent her home to put socks on. My friend told her daughter not to take any notice of her teacher, so the kid went back to school and said, 'My mommy said I'm not to take any notice of you!' You have to be careful.

MARGARET I just had a thought, that maybe the women here who are having trouble accepting the fact that they have to kind of 'get down' with their babies, and spend so much time with them, and are finding it difficult—because they are wondering about who they are and their career and so on—maybe it's because they are older.

MORGAN This is true. This is all part of the fact that my generation, we are just pre-taking-the-Pill. In fact, I did start taking the Pill, but it was too late. I was thinking, God, even the Pill failed me. But it is one of these things, if your heart isn't in it, it won't work. Being older is an issue.

MARGARET What about infanticide in England?

MORGAN I can give you a little bridge. I was thinking about that world I was living in, the One O'Clock Club. They would sit there smoking, and I was feeling quite sorry for myself sometimes because of our poverty, because my husband was a painter, and we had hardly any money. It was so exhausting, and I was thinking, Most of this is because of being poor. I could buy myself a baby-sitter, I could buy myself out to some degree, but I was worried about basic things. Were we eating well enough? Of course we were, but I worried. In the middle of all this, I knew we'd made a kind of vow of poverty—if we were going to be artists, we were going to be poor. Lots of artists aren't, but you run a higher chance. Whereas a lot of these women at the One O'Clock Club had no way out. This wasn't their choice to be poor, and living in this slum. They couldn't say, 'I'm sick of this. I think I'll go to Prince George and be a teacher.' We even had the hope that we might sell something, but with them it was just the drudgery, and they didn't have any outlets at all. They could perhaps take their children to daycare and get a job wiping tables, that was about it.

Some of them had such terrible home lives, with violent husbands—I don't mean they were battered, but there was a level of aggression and tension that they lived with all the time. They used to slap their kids a lot, and it was abuse, but it was just part of the tough way. You couldn't baby the kids. It was a kind of decision, a way of dealing with this trapped life. I was amazed at some of the spirit and humour of these women, and touched by their wit.

At the same time, this was a place in London where there were a lot of Council estates. Some of them were really rough. There was a high rate of infanticide. I noticed that in the national news: a baby would be killed. There seemed to be a high risk among poor women living on these Council estates, because the estates had broken up traditional communities, Cockney communities, women no longer lived near their mothers. They felt isolated living so high up off the ground. People here pay to live off the ground, but in London, you pay to put your feet on the ground.

The news would report, 'In Abervalley House last week …,' and I would know that building. It was in a certain area, that certain kinds of conditions and stress contributed to the incidence of infanticide. No matter what kinds of neurotic goings on there are in the middle classes, I think it doesn't compare with actual, physical stress, tension, isolation, and poverty—which was general to that whole community. It was not advertised very widely, because it was the responsibility of the state for that not to happen. It's easy to say, 'Oh, that person is neurotic because his mother or his father were abused'—but if you say it was because they lived in these terrible slums we built for them, which we don't do anything about ... We found our own families, our own sisters, aunts, grandmas among the people in the community.

MARGARET Through the hut, through the One O'Clock Club. It was the saving grace.

MORGAN Yes, and when my kids did go to school, the schools were very good. It was like an extension of the One O'Clock Club. Women were very involved in the school. They had more authority. Just because someone had gone to university and taken a course in education didn't mean they were going to tell them something, which I think is very healthy—and the fact that lots of the mothers and grannies were playground helps and dinner ladies.

MARGARET Eyes right inside.

MORGAN Yes, and they were being paid for it. It wasn't volunteer like here, which always produces a selection of people who have free time and money, whereas these women just had to do work, and this was the best way to do it.

MARGARET To get back to infanticide ...

MORGAN That was my basic fear when I had a baby. That's what I said earlier on, that I was frightened as to how I was going to keep this baby alive. It's very exciting having a baby, but with the shock of a new life, its opposite appears—death, the cycle of death. You have been responsible for this amazing thing, for bringing this child to life, now you have to keep it alive.

Mr. Mom
Motherhood Expresses Me Beautifully

Guy Allen, born in 1947 in Colorado Springs, Colorado
Male Mother of Derek, Pierce, and Tait
Interviewed by Susan Swan

SUSAN Guy, I am testing the recorder. What colour of underwear do you have on?

GUY I have no underwear on.

SUSAN None. Okay. What are your early images of motherhood?

GUY My mother was a housewife and somebody I completely identified with. I wanted to be like her, and she was somebody who I could talk to. We had a secret world we shared. My father was excluded from that world. We saw him as someone to get around, someone to avoid. We presented him with the images that he wanted to see, just to keep him out of our way.

SUSAN How is it that you have come to see yourself as a mother now? You are how old?

GUY I'm 44. I say to my kids, 'Now I am 40 fucking four.'

SUSAN And how many children do you have at '40 fucking four'?

GUY I have Derek, a 20-year-old; Pierce, a 19-year-old; and a year ago I adopted Tait, a three-year-old who is now four.

SUSAN That seems like a big step to take when you've just finished with two children.

GUY Yes, I thought the next big step in my life was being rid of my kids and exploring myself creatively without them, but I met this kid through a friend who became my lover, and this kid was having a lot of problems.

SUSAN What kind of problems?

GUY He was violent, he was angry, he was unhappy, he cried a lot, and life was difficult for him, and he made it difficult for everybody around him.

SUSAN This inspired you to take an interest in him? To

become his legal stepfather?

GUY Yes. I started by taking Tait to my house on his own. I'd say to his mother, 'Let me take him off your hands for a day or two.' His mother was in fairly rough shape. She was having a hard time coping with the basics, and she felt guilty about the kid. She felt she had done badly with him, and she was unable to stand up to his angry assaults on her. If I had not had experience with children, I would have stayed away from him—he would have been frightening to me. Instead, I thought I recognized something of myself in him, because I was an angry child, too.

SUSAN Does that mean that you'll be involved in Tait's life from now on?

GUY That's correct. I made that commitment. He has a room in my house, although I don't live with his mother. My other sons, Derek and Pierce, have strong maternal instincts, and they both participate in raising him. I still get to take vacations and do things I want, because they step in and help.

SUSAN You are the only woman-identified man I've ever met. Can you tell me how you came to identify yourself as a mother?

GUY Well, I didn't like fathers, because my own father beat me. I identified with girls, and at the playground at school, I spent a lot of my time talking to them. They seemed to be the only people who made any sense to me.

SUSAN What made sense to you about girls?

GUY We talked seriously about things boys joked around about, and there was always something intimidating about boys to me. I just didn't want to be around them. I met exceptions, but the exceptions were not considered real males. They were considered weirdos, like me. I couldn't make contact with the mainstream male.

SUSAN Tell me more about the secret world you shared with your mother? What was so wonderful about that secret world?

GUY It was a private world in which we understood each other. There was a lot of acceptance in that world. We just kind of knew what each other was thinking and feeling. We were always trying to make life more comfortable for each other, at least this was the way I perceived it. I considered my mother somebody who was very smart, and I saw my father as somebody who thought he was smart—he was a moron who thought he was smart—but I thought he was an idiot.

SUSAN So you saw your mother as a strong figure, a kind of role model?

GUY Yes, my mother was a figure of strength. My father was a figure of weakness. I didn't want to be like my father, because I never wanted to be weak like that. I never wanted to have to prop up my self-image with falsehoods.

SUSAN And dominating other people?

GUY Appearing to dominate people. I don't think he really succeeded in dominating us. In fact, he failed to dominate my mother or me or anybody else.

SUSAN When did you first think of having a child?

GUY After my first son was born. My first child was conceived amongst the haze and exhilaration produced by booze and drugs and the Rolling Stones back in the sixties. My wife and I just failed to get birth control together. In fact, it was after I had separated from my wife that I found out she was pregnant.

SUSAN How did you feel about that news?

GUY At that time, I was in trouble with the FBI in the United States, over the draft. I was crumbling psychologically, I was about to have a major nervous breakdown—I could see it happening, but I didn't know what it was.

SUSAN When did it strike you that you were a father, or a mother-inspired father?

GUY I started out very badly with my kids. Six months after the first child was born, I had a complete nervous breakdown. I couldn't sleep past five in the morning. Whenever I went into the bathroom and saw myself in the mirror, I'd throw up. I felt an intense self-loathing. At that time, my wife was taking care of both the child and me—she had two children to take care of. One of them was six months old, one of them was six-foot-three—that was me. I was a burden, I was a hassle to her. I even caught myself in an act of violence with my son. I threw a book at him from across the room.

SUSAN You had temporarily become your father.

GUY I had stumbled into a situation where I was behaving like him, and that was horrifying.

SUSAN When did this begin to change?

GUY We conceived a second child. I don't know quite how, because we were never really living together steadily, but we did have sex. I became involved in therapy, I was on anti-depressant drugs for three years. At one point, when the kids were three and two years old, I abandoned my wife and children and just went to Europe. I was there in search of some kind of meaning, and I was sitting at a table in a café on a Greek Island, and it dawned on me that if my life was to mean anything, I would find it with my sons back in Toronto. I announced to my wife that I wanted to take care of my sons. She thought that was a good laugh. She didn't believe it, and I don't blame her for not believing it. Within six weeks of my return, I became treasurer at the parent co-op daycare centre that I had never even seen before.

SUSAN You immediately got involved on your return?

GUY I plunged in. It was really, really hard. You cannot imagine the terror with which I regarded this daycare centre.

SUSAN How did you see it?

GUY Just the idea of going there and not knowing what to do with all these children—I thought all these people would be looking at me and judging me and thinking how terrible I was.

SUSAN Because you had gone to Europe and then abandoned your family, so to speak?

GUY Because I had, yes. And so I actually started keeping my sons on my own, I began making a relationship with them away from my wife, and I really enjoyed taking care of them. It didn't matter whether I was changing their diapers or what I was doing. It felt better and more solid to me than anything else I had done in my life. Then my wife had problems around this time and was willing to have me be the primary parent. It was at this point that I really solidified my relations with them.

SUSAN You had almost full custody of them?

GUY Yes.

SUSAN What age were they then?

GUY I had almost full custody from the time they were around four and three.

SUSAN Now, I have been in your house, and I know it to be a most unusual home. It is a household full of men raising men. Can you tell me a little bit about how that structure worked practically, when your kids were little?

GUY I was living with Arnie Achtman. Arnie and I weren't as close as we are now, but we have been living together for 17 years now. Then, we had just been together for a while. It was an undefined relationship, and his involvement with the children was at first nil, and he gradually did begin taking a part in raising them. One of the reasons why it worked as well as it did is that it grew naturally. It wasn't something we made to fit a model. Often people in their marriage or love relationships create artificial situations where somebody is suddenly in a situation to raise children, and they didn't know the children ahead of time.

SUSAN So you arrived at a pretty stable and definitive structure through a natural evolution. I remember your house. There were always meals on time, there was always shopping done, the house might have been in disarray at times, but it was clean and relatively organized whenever I was over there. How did that happen?

GUY Well, I was the mother. I saw to it that it happened—it was I who did that. That's not to say Arnie didn't contribute; he did a lot. My definition of a mother is the person who constitutes the fall-back position. A mother is the person who is there when nobody else is and when all other systems have failed, and so I took responsibility for seeing that the kids were taken care of.

SUSAN Can you expand on this?

GUY It wasn't just a matter of taking care of kids. I felt intense anger about my own upbringing. This anger stopped me and everything I tried to do creatively. Raising my own children turned out to be a way of discharging this anger and of acting creatively on it, and I had, with Derek and Pierce, a remarkably positive and happy relationship. We had good times together, we enjoyed ourselves. I always had the feeling that good times were part of a good house, because I was very sensitive to having come from a house with a lot of bad things all the time.

Every night we would come home from the daycare quite exhausted. While they were in the bathtub, I'd fix dinner, and then they'd come down, and they would have dinner, then we'd play music together. We'd turn on rock 'n roll and get out the pots and pans and bang on them. Everybody laughed a lot, everybody had fun, they called me 'Guy,' they didn't call me 'Dad.' I had never liked being called 'Dad' because of my association with my own father.

SUSAN You are a man, though. How do you think your experience as a mother differs from that of women?

GUY Oh, this is significant because, especially at the time when I was raising my kids, I received recognition that women don't get—because I was a man doing it, I got support. Everybody that came to my house, including you, everybody said, 'Wow, this is amazing. This is really incredible,' and yet I was doing what mothers do.

SUSAN I remember you giving me the best piece of advice about mothering I have ever had. You said that the best thing I could do for a child was to forget my guilt trip and live my life so I was enjoying it, and in that way I would be a good role model.

GUY Yes, I have another way of putting that piece of advice. That is, if you are walking along with your child and you see a mud puddle, just make sure that you, the mother, are the first one in it. [*laughter*] If you find yourself in the role of worrying about the child jumping into the puddle, and—even worse—terrorizing the child about jumping into the puddle, it's time to make a change. I was always crazier than my kids. I always wanted to be the discipline problem in the house, and I still am. My kids still worry about how I am going to behave, and I think that works fairly well.

SUSAN What *was* your discipline system?

GUY Well, quite early, my discipline system was to be unpredictable and inconsistent.

SUSAN That goes against everything you read in books about child-raising. They say you are supposed to be consistent.

GUY I think consistency is the worst thing you can do for a child. What are you going to do? Present them with a situation that they will never meet again in their whole life? I always tried to keep mine guessing. I wanted them to never know what to expect, yet there were times when I got depressed and had a hard time as a parent, times when we got into ruts.

SUSAN When they got into ruts?

GUY When I got into a rut. You know, what's significant about being a parent is that you, as a parent, are responsible for what happens. If there are bad times coming down, what's your four year old going to do about it? You are the one who has to do something about it. It is clearly your role to alter it. To get mad at your child because your child is having a bad time is counter-productive.

SUSAN And yet women carry around so much guilt and blame as the one who makes everything go wrong.

GUY Yes. You know, I think if I had been a woman, I probably wouldn't want to be a mother—because it would have been expected of me, and my rut would have been pre-made. I never had that feeling of a rut, because for me raising children was probably the most creative, dynamic, revolutionary act that a man could commit at the time that I did it.

SUSAN I think that's true. The men's movement has caused a lot of rethinking in this area. I'm thinking of Robert Bly and the redefinition of masculinity that's going on.

GUY I'm not sure that this is a real men's movement yet. A lot of the fathers I observe now—especially those in the middle classes—are more involved in their children's lives, but a lot of them seem emasculated—like they traded in their masculinity—and I am not sure you have to do that.

SUSAN You haven't done that?

GUY No, I have always had the fantasy of wanting to be a caring male mother parent for my kids and yet wanting to be a fully present sexual being, doing all of the things that I, as a man, want to do. So I have never wanted to see the parental role as a limiting one, as setting up a bunch of things that I don't do. I do a lot of things with kids that shock other people.

SUSAN Can you give me an example?

GUY Like my four year old, he's full of aggression—this has been one of his difficulties. He comes home from daycare cursing. He'll come out and swear on the subway, he'll yell at you—'Fuck you,'—right? I curse back in these long chains of things that I make up. Then he starts laughing and then he makes up another long chain.

SUSAN Like an old-fashioned Greek curse against the gods?

GUY Oh no, no, his are down-home gutter curses. 'You fuckin' asshole twit,'—you know—and then, we go at it like that, and then we are both sitting there laughing at the end of it, and his swearing has lost all its power—or he'll say something like, 'I hate you,' and I stick my tongue out at him.

SUSAN So you defuse his anger by turning it into play?

GUY Yes, and I also don't want to let him monopolize all the freedom, and this is what I find kids do with parents. They'll try to corner you. The parent is in the position of saying what should happen and giving a kid rational reasons for everything, and the parent gets isolated in the position of rationality, and reason is one of the worst positions you can be in in your life. To retain your freedom, you have to be able to do anything, at any minute, that you feel like doing. I know some parents who can make this work in private but who can't make it work in front of other people, because they feel like they have to behave in a decorous fashion in public. Kids will use that. Kids have a real sense of their powerlessness, and they'll look for occasions where they can manipulate situations to get power—and I don't blame them.

SUSAN Yes, I don't blame them either. Do you discipline this boy in any way? Does he ever do anything you feel you must come down hard on him for?

GUY I never had to discipline my older two, it never came up, but Tait has to be dealt with, and Tait becomes violent sometimes, and we have to use force.

SUSAN What kind of force?

GUY Well, you have to physically overpower him, which in the case of a four-year-old is not hard—you just pick him up. If he calls for more discipline, we manage to give him time out in a room by himself, to think things through, and sometimes I get physical with him—I will grab him in a way that he really knows I mean business. He's tough. He's a real challenge, but he's partly a challenge because he's got an incredible spirit and a strong sense of his rights. He's smart. I respect that a lot.

SUSAN What's a typical day with Tait like?

GUY [*laughs*] Is any day with Tait typical, is the question. We get up around seven o'clock, and I get him dressed or he dresses himself. He is very independent. Then we head out on the transit together. I either get him breakfast at my place or go to the muffin shop, and I buy a *Globe and Mail* and sit there and drink coffee while he eats one of those huge muffins they make there.

SUSAN You can actually read a newspaper while your kid is right there? I'm astonished. How can you do that?

GUY With every child the relationship is different, but with each of mine we've had a great deal of separateness in our relations, so that even when we were together, we were rather quiet—and we don't always talk a lot. There are periods when we are sitting across the table from each other and not saying anything for 10 minutes, and he's often doing his thing, and maybe I'm reading the newspaper for a while.

SUSAN My experience as a mother is that small children go into a kind of a panic if I am mentally distracted, and I am wondering if it's because you are a man that you are better able to disengage when you are with a child, more than, say, I would have been with my daughter Samantha or with my ex-boyfriend's son Tyler.

GUY I've tried to figure out why that is and whether or not it is a function of a woman's feeling guilty about taking time to herself, which no doubt these kids can pick up really easily. It may be. I, as a man—now that you mention it—I have always had a strong sense of the importance of standing up for my rights with the kids. People ask me about discipline behaviour. I've never really bothered kids much about how I think they should behave—I've never bothered them about brushing their teeth, for instance. My primary discipline with kids involves protecting my own rights, so I can have peace of mind and a life that's separate from theirs.

I find kids are ready to accept this kind of discipline, because it's rationally based. It's not based on a belief about their behaviour—on any notions about what kind of human beings they should be. Parents dream up all sorts of notions like this, for example, that a kid should sit in that chair with his hands folded and have proper posture. It's not anything like that. It's like, look—you have to leave me alone now because it is my right. Your needs are taken care of, and I need some time by myself. When that is counterbalanced by a respect for their rights, discipline works naturally. A lot of parents have problems realizing that their children have rights. It's always easy to overrun their rights.

SUSAN As a woman and a mother, I felt that my child had rights but I didn't, and I am sure that many mothers do feel this. That our rights are secondary to the needs of the child—and this is true biologically at a certain stage, when the children are very small, but it seems to get carried on into their childhood.

GUY Even when my kids were quite young, I remember feeling that I had rights. Now this may be that I was quite young, too. You have to realize that, right at the same time I started raising my sons, I was beginning a process of psychoanalysis which lasted for 20 years. This was basically a process of self-reconstruction. I was starting from point zero. Everything I had been up to the age of 23 was invalidated, and I didn't want to carry anything over. I carried no friend, no contact, no nothing, over from that period. I wanted to start over—I was very much a blank slate. I wasn't much ahead of the kids, except that I was bigger and had money and was in charge. I didn't really feel like I knew a lot.

SUSAN You are saying essentially that you gave birth to yourself as you were raising your children?

GUY Yes, I felt like they were guiding me. They always seemed wise and able to understand basic things that I had forgotten and was trying to get back to—I always respected their ways of looking at things. What they had to say to me about me was really positive. One of the things that a single parent sometimes experiences with children, especially a single parent who is oppressed by economic circumstances, is that the kids often take on a role of helping the parent out. For instance, I remember being depressed, and I remember the kids telling me how valuable I was, how I was just feeling bad temporarily and that I would get over it, but that, for their purposes, I was just as valuable as ever I was.

SUSAN You didn't feel guilty about laying your emotional problems on your children? I think a woman might be told this. I was told this—that because I was feeling emotionally low, I was somehow victimizing my kids.

GUY I didn't feel that way.

SUSAN I didn't think so. Let's go back to the day with Tait—we're eating muffins and reading the newspaper. At least he's eating muffins, and you're reading the newspaper. What happens after that?

GUY I take him to the daycare at St. George and Bloor. Then I go to my work at the university.

SUSAN What time do you drop him off at daycare?

GUY Usually between 8:00 and 9:00. It often happens that I take him in, and his mother picks him up, or vice versa, but on a day where I both drop him off and pick him up, I would get him between 5:00 and 6:00. I always experience a period of excitement before I pick him up, of really wanting to see him and being excited about what we are going to do, I find that a real release from the problems of the adult world—deadlines for manuscripts and everything like that. I forget about all this and just get into what's for dinner, and reading him a story, and going to bed. I have found, from talking to a number of mothers, that they don't feel this positive sense of, Oh great, I'm going to see my child—some of them haven't experienced that.

SUSAN I don't think many of them ever experience that.

GUY Some of them do, and yet I can see that if somebody imposed on me the obligation of being a mother, I wouldn't experience the thrill I experience because I chose to be a mother. It expresses me beautifully that I do this, but I wouldn't do that if I had it imposed upon me.

SUSAN Yes, I understand. What happens when you bring Tait home? You go home on the subway?

GUY We go home on the subway. We joke around on the subway, and we get home, and I sit him down and give him dinner, which I do not eat with him. It's against my principles to eat with children. I give him his food and relate to him by sitting down and talking to him about what kind of a day he had and things like that. Then he gets up and runs around the house for a while and starts playing, and then I get him to take a bath. He always likes me to get in the bathtub with him. I don't always do it, but he says, 'Why don't you take a bath with me?' We get in the bathtub and we play around in there for a while, and then I usually have him in bed by 7:00, which is quite early. I read him a story, and I lie on the bed with him as I read the story, and he says, 'Why don't you stay here for another minute?' I usually do that—and then it's good night, and I'm gone. He's free to do what he wants for as late as he wants, as long as he stays in his room, but my dealings with him are over at that time.

I presented this to him as a question of my rights. 'I have given you what I am going to give you today, and I can't wait to see you tomorrow morning. I am very excited about that, but for now I am finished.' As soon as I put him to bed, a wave of tiredness comes over me—I can't even hold a conversation on the phone until nine o'clock or 9:30. That indicates to me the intensity of the energy that's been going on with him, so I always try to relax after he's in bed.

SUSAN What happens if he has a problem in his room alone? Do you come in and intercede?

GUY Of course, but I am pretty tough with him. Once I am sure that his needs are taken care of, I don't get soft and take him into my arms and say, 'Oh, you can come downstairs with me now, and spend another hour and a half harassing me.' I would do that if I saw he was emotionally upset, or if I saw something that was really different and unusual, but on the whole—and this makes me different from a lot of mothers that I see—I don't get pushed once I have a sense that he's been fairly dealt with. He goes to bed at 7:00, and his eyes are usually closed by 7:30.

SUSAN Can you give an example of a situation where he would require more attention after this seven o'clock time period?

GUY He might engineer something in the room that would require me to come up. There would be a crash—or maybe he would be crying—and I would go up there, and then I would perceive that there was something special about it, that he was really upset, and maybe he just needs me to hold him for a few minutes.

SUSAN So it's a snap judgment. You assess his state of mind.

GUY Yes. On the other hand, I never like to suggest to a child that I can do more for the child than I can. I can't remove the world's sadness for a child. This is something they have to deal with, and I have to deal with too. I can't promise to make the world better than it is. I can't promise to deal with their own emotional problems. They have to deal with them. So I don't promise a child things that are outside my control, and I try to suggest to children that they are responsible for their own emotional lives.

Actually, I spend a lot of time with Tait on this—on getting very sad, down, and angry, and negative—and I point out to him that, 'You can change this, Tait. Only you can do it, and you have to decide to be happy,' and it's been remarkable. I started with teaching him this when he was about two-and-a-half. I said, 'You know, you are unhappy a lot of the time. You can decide to change it. You can't change it all the time, but you can change it a lot of the time, just by deciding.' I've found, as the cliché goes, children learn so much faster than any adult. It takes adults years of working on a process like that to learn it. Kids are much more receptive to it.

SUSAN He didn't realize he had that choice.

GUY No, he thought he had to be sad. He thought that was the way it was, because he was born at a time when his mother was just sad all the time, and her sadness was all he knew.

Children have to feel secure, they have to feel their basic needs will be taken care of, but I feel that, even at a very early age, the right thing to do is to suggest to the child that the child bears primary responsibility for his or her own happiness, and that it is not something I am equipped to provide. My mother suggested to me that she could somehow make me happy—and it was horrible when I had to go it on my own. I lacked the skills to make myself happy, because I'd had such a close devoted relationship with my mother.

SUSAN What have been your biggest problems as a parent? In this style of parenting which you've invented.

GUY When he was 11 and 12, my oldest son, Derek, had terrible, terrible migraines. These migraines lasted for up to four weeks at a time, with him lying on the bed with the most incredibly pathetic expression on his face, and I finally realized and accepted that there was nothing I could do about this. That I had to resume my life, I had to leave him there alone with his headache—that everything that could be done about his headaches had been done, and that I had to get on with things and let it go. Those headaches were painful.

SUSAN What happened to the headaches? How did that resolve itself?

GUY One day he had his last headache. It was unbelievable. They just ended. He also made a big change. He had appeared to be somebody who was going to be very unhappy. I felt some mother's guilt, because after he was born, I'd had my breakdown, and it took him many, many years to trust me. For a long time, he never really trusted me, and he was abusive with his mother. I thought he was going to be somebody with a nagging, whining, undermining personality. All in all, he was a difficult child up to the age of 14, and then everything changed. I admire very much who he is now and what he represents. His attitude toward other people is exemplary. He is kind, he is easy-going.

SUSAN What brought about this change? Were your methods of child-raising sinking in?

GUY I don't give myself any credit for it. I think, as a parent, that his example is a good one to think about. You have to allow them to go through what they are going to go through, and I see parents panic about these things like migraine headaches or emotional problems. The child can go through 10 years of emotional problems and come out the other side okay.

Many people predicted when I was a child that I was going to end up in prison—and I did come close—but despite what the literature on parenting and a lot of the talk that I hear around suggests, parents can't do more than they can. Children are independent beings. They're going to go through what they are going to go through. I've always felt that the best thing a parent can do is live a good life, and then a child can see what that is. That a parent could be happy and have their kids and do things that are interesting to them. You can't control your child's life, and the world's full of unhappy, difficult things, and if you spare them all that, it's just phony and artificial anyway. They're going to go through it and it's hard to watch, but you have to accept they are going to do this, and you can only make it worse sometimes by giving it too much attention, or—

SUSAN Or trying to save them.

GUY You have to give problems what attention you can, and then let the children go their own way. Now, I am not saying you neglect problems—although people often ask me, 'What's your secret to parenting?' and I say, 'Neglect is my secret.'

SUSAN Tell me a little bit about Derek and Pierce now. What they are doing, and what sort of people they are?

GUY I am stunned by them as people, and I am very pleased. They are both still living with me at a time when many of their friends have moved out—and there is a lot of conflict amongst their friends, and their parents report back to me, and I hear about this. My house is sort of a refuge.

SUSAN How old are they?

GUY Derek and Pierce are 20 and 19. They are very kind, gentle, manly men. They're smart, and they're nice people to be around. They make a lot of jokes at my expense, but they love me, and they treat me with respect, and they help me raise Tait. I just went on holiday with Tait's mother for nine days and left Tait with Pierce with complete confidence. Tait has a better time with Derek and Pierce than he would have if I were there. It's really funny, because I see my kids treat Tait the same way I treat them. They've just copied me. They show the same mix of respect and consideration and kindness and toughness. The toughness comes in when they protect their own rights. They know that just because a child is four years old doesn't mean he has a right to destroy all the objects in the room.

SUSAN And their aspirations?

GUY Derek and Pierce are both rock 'n' roll musicians. They are very good musicians, and they just came out of the studio with a demo tape for their band. They both work in the Big Carrot, which is Toronto's primary health-food store. One of them is a butcher, and the other one works in the vegetable department.

They still regard me as a behaviour problem. I have a funny story to tell. One day, about a month ago, I got a phone call at the university and a voice said, 'Hi, Guy.' I said, 'Hi, who's this?' 'It's Pierce.' 'Oh Pierce, how you doing?' I didn't recognize his voice, because Pierce has never ever called me at the university. And he said, 'How are you doing?' 'Oh, I'm doing alright, how are you?' 'Oh, I'm doing fine, I guess. So what's happening?' 'Well, I don't know what's happening, Pierce, I'm just sitting here doing my work.' 'What do you think you are going to be doing tonight?' Pierce asked. 'I don't know, I haven't given it any thought.' 'Do you think you are going to be around the house?' I told him I hadn't made any plans.

Then I said, 'Pierce, what's going on here? What do you want to know about? Do you want me around the house tonight or out of the house? Which is it?'—I thought he might want to have a talk with me or have a party. And he said, 'Oh well, it's not exactly that.' 'So what's going on?' 'Well, I'm thinking of having somebody over for dinner, and I just wanted to make sure there wouldn't be a conflict. I thought you might be having somebody over for dinner.' I said, 'No. No problem. Who are you having over for dinner, Pierce?' 'Oh, just a woman named Ellen.' 'Oh, you mean this is somebody that you're in love with?' 'Well, sort of.' So I asked, 'Would you like me to stay away?' 'Oh, no, no, no problem.' Then I said, 'Oh, I know what you want me to do. You want me to behave.' And he said, 'Well, yeah. She's really shy, you know, she might not understand some of the things that you usually do.'

I came in that night, and Pierce was there with Ellen, and I said, 'Hi, Ellen, I'm Guy,' and then two minutes later I said, 'Ellen, it was nice to meet you. I'll see you later. So long, Pierce.' I was gone, and that was it. The next morning, I was sitting in the kitchen having a cup of coffee, and Pierce came up to me, put his arms around me, and said, 'Guy, I just want you to know that I was really proud of you last night.'

SUSAN That's a great story. One last question—a philosophical one. What do you think has to happen before mothering can be something that women can do more profitably, and maybe men, too?

GUY Well, I think this has to be answered in the same way that I would answer any philosophical question about life. Mothering has to be taken out of the puritanical realm. Motherhood should be about making free and clear choices: I am doing this because I choose to do it. We have to accept the fact that raising children is just a piece of life. Life is defeat and sadness and has difficulty in it, and child-raising is a parent's responsibility—but the way a child turns out or reacts is not solely due to the parent.

For example, I have no doubt that when my son was having those terrible migraines some people concluded that there was something about my parenting that was causing them. Maybe some people said I was too strict. Maybe some people said I was too easy or neglected my children. But I really don't believe that. We need to recognize the kids as independent beings and ourselves as independent beings. That for a period of about 20 years, we are sharing an environment and sharing a life, and that we have chosen the situation. It's a choice that has a wonderful and incredible positive potential, and it's not about making up a list of rules that one should and should not do.

Guatemalan Midwife

From Village Life to Big City Blues

Izabel Martinez, born in 1959 in San Miguel Acatan, Guatemala
Mother of Cecibel, Mary, Pedro, and Juanito
Interviewed by Margaret Dragu

MARGARET When did you first want to have a baby?

IZABEL When I was 15. I liked babies when I was young. I always carried my brother and sister. I said, 'Someday I will have a baby.'

MARGARET Did you help to raise them when you were little?

IZABEL Yes, because my mother was really sick.

MARGARET How many brothers and sisters?

IZABEL I had five brothers and two sisters.

MARGARET While you were taking care of your brothers and sisters, your mother was doing what?

IZABEL Preparing the food, washing the clothes by hand. Because we didn't have a tap, we had to fetch water. I stayed behind with my little sister and brother.

MARGARET Were you living on a farm with your mother and your father?

IZABEL We lived in a small town of twenty thousand people.

MARGARET In the mountainous area of Guatemala?

IZABEL Yes, in the mountains.

MARGARET You have four children. How old were you when you had your first one?

IZABEL Twenty-four. I had her in Guatemala.

MARGARET What was the difference between having a baby in Guatemala and your last baby, a son in Canada?

IZABEL In Guatemala, we have babies at home, because we don't have a hospital close to us. I had to find a midwife.

MARGARET And later, you yourself became a midwife. How many babies have you helped into the world in Guatemala?

IZABEL More than a hundred, I think.

MARGARET Having a baby at home must feel very different

to having it in a hospital.

IZABEL It is different, because we don't have pregnancy tests and medical check-ups every month, and everything like that. For my last baby, I wanted more safety, so that if something happened to me, I'd have everything around me. At home, if something goes wrong, you have in your mind that the baby will die, because you don't have easy transportation. The hospital is far away. But if you have faith in yourself, everything is easy.

MARGARET Did you worry more in Guatemala when you were pregnant, or did you worry more here?

IZABEL My faith is with babies. In Canada, I was worried because I had problems with my cervix, and I had to go to the doctor every week or two weeks, but there I went to the doctor maybe three times during my pregnancy.

MARGARET When you were helping in Guatemala, what did you do if there was a problem, if, say, the woman was bleeding?

IZABEL My group of pregnant ladies came every week to the clinic where I was working, and I knew how everything was going, because I was checking them. If something was wrong, I advised them to go to the hospital the day before delivery. Many ladies didn't like to go, but if they were bleeding, I tried to send them to the hospital, or advised them to stay in bed.

MARGARET When you had your first baby, did it seem different from expected, a surprise?

IZABEL No, it wasn't. Half of what happened I already knew. When my mother's children cried, I didn't know what to do, I gave them back to her, but when mine cried, they were my responsibility. It wasn't a big adjustment for me, because I was already working in the hospital with babies, but that responsibility was surprising—to change diapers and feed my own baby.

MARGARET When you had your first baby, your relatives were around you still?

IZABEL They used to live in the same house. Now, with Juan, I feel that everybody takes care of him, my niece, my nephew, my daughter. My daughter is helping a lot.

MARGARET But what about privacy? Do you want to work again or stay home?

IZABEL I would like to stay at home with him, of course. It depends on whether my sister-in-law will stay at home, because daycare is expensive. What I earn would just pay daycare, in which case, I would rather look after him.

MARGARET In Guatemala, you would never have to think about daycare?

IZABEL When I had my first baby, I left her at home with my sister and my mother, knowing they would take care of her as well as I would. It's different here than there.

MARGARET It is harder to keep the extended family together here than there?

IZABEL Yes, it is hard, because my niece, for example, wants to learn English. She wants to continue studying, so she can't stay at home to take care of him. My sister-in-law also wants to learn English.

MARGARET It is so expensive here for rent and food, more people have to work.

IZABEL In our town in Guatemala, we owned a house, fruit trees—we were almost self-sufficient. Salt was all we had to buy. But here ... When I was working in that clinic, I got 70 *quetzales* a month, subsistence wages, but I lived with my father. I paid him for my corn, he only needed to buy meat and cloth, and 70 *quetzales* was enough. Here, 70 *quetzales* is only enough for one or two days' worth of groceries.

MARGARET It's a longer distance too, to travel, to visit.

IZABEL Yes, if you have a car here, you are fortunate, but a car is expensive, it makes you spend money.

MARGARET Do you find raising your children as they get older also very different here?

IZABEL Yes, here, when they go to school, they see many children who have more things or clothes. In Guatemala, everybody is poor too, so everyone is the same. It is hard for us when our children ask for expensive things, like clothes. Sometimes Marie wants to have something and asks if we can go and buy it. I say, 'No, we can't.' In Guatemala, you have two pairs of clothes, maybe one.

MARGARET What about keeping up their Spanish?

IZABEL We mix Spanish with English. When the children are together with others, they speak just English, even at home. When they are alone with us, they use some English and some Spanish. I think they may be missing out on Spanish. I hope not.

MARGARET You try to speak to them in Spanish?

IZABEL Yes, all the time.

MARGARET Are they learning your own Indian language?

IZABEL Maria can speak it. Pedro understands it, but he doesn't speak it.

MARGARET Whenever I visit here, it feels like all your whole family likes to be here.

IZABEL I think so, because our whole family lives in the same town, and we like staying together.

MARGARET I've wanted advice about raising babies Aretha's age—almost two—because I find it hard to keep her from hitting, scratching, breaking things—to say no. You are very gentle with your children. How do you do that?

IZABEL Always remember you can't do very much—because they're growing. You have to be patient. If the child wants to do something, and you'd rather he didn't, you can say no or give something to the child to do, give him a toy.

My sister-in-law was not a nice mother. She hit her children, and when they were five years old, the boy was very bad because she hit him so much. He liked to hit everybody. You have to be careful when they are that age. In my opinion, when a boy or girl does something very bad, you can maybe hit his hand, maybe once. I didn't hit my children, but one day, when Pedro was five years old, I hit him, just once. It was amazing. I cried afterward. He understood.

MARGARET When you hit them too much they just get angry.

IZABEL I know. But if you give too much to them, it's bad too. When Cecibel was young, everybody gave things to her, but a friend told me, 'Don't give so much to her, because when she is older she will ask for more,' and I said, 'Okay, I'll stop and pay more attention to her.' You have to have patience. That's it.

In Guatemala we have a big place, and the weather's not cold. The children can go out to play with other children—and maybe their own brother or sister can watch. It's very easy, but here, they can't go out, and the house is too little. They have to be careful of the stairs, and so on. My mother-in-law used to sit outside and watch Pedro. 'Go and do what you want to do. I will stay with him,' she would say. But my mother-in-law is not here. My mother is here, but sometimes she stays with my sister or my brother. In Guatemala, it is easy for the grandparent to watch them. It wasn't hard for me.

When we went to Florida, Pedro was one-and-a-half years old. Cecibel, who was about eight years old, took care of him while we worked. We were gone from 7:00 a.m. to 5:00 or 7:00 at night. There were snakes in Florida, and Cecibel was very scared when she saw the snakes.

MARGARET It is colder here, but not as dangerous. Will you all continue living together in the future?

IZABEL I was talking with Cecibel on Monday. She said that she would always take me with her. 'I don't think so, ' I said, 'because you will marry a Canadian man. He won't allow me to be with you.'

MARGARET How does that make you feel?

IZABEL Very bad. I like to have my family close. When we were in Mexico, everybody came to visit us. When I was in Guatemala, people came to us. I love that, but my children don't. Life here is different.

MARGARET I have a picture of an Indian family with 40 people—the grandmother at home with the family, not in an old-age home. I see my own mother maybe once a year. She likes being alone.

IZABEL It is very sad. I experienced it with old people when I was living in Richmond. One lady said that her daughter comes once a week for 10 minutes. I think my children will be close, but my grandchildren may not be.

MARGARET Do you dream about going back to Guatemala?

IZABEL Yes, all the time. My hope, my dream, is to go back.

Going It Alone

A Handful and a Footful

Renee Rodin, born in 1945 in Montreal, Quebec
Mother of Joey, Noah, and Daniel
Interviewed by Margaret Dragu

MARGARET When did you first want to have a baby?

RENEE I never thought very consciously about actually having children. I enjoyed playing with dolls, as a kid, but didn't think about being a mother after that. I really didn't plan my kids. One minute I didn't have them, the next I did. Also, I'd been with the same person since we were both 16, and he was into being a father. Neither of us was very aware. Years after I had my children, I suddenly one day remembered my mother saying to me—very often, from the time I'd hit puberty—that all she wanted was to become a grandmother. She'd say, "I don't care from who, just make me a grandmother." I think a lot of my becoming a mother was a subconscious desire to make my own mother happy. In fact, it didn't work for her, but I'm glad I had them.

MARGARET How old are your children? Did they come quickly?

RENEE I had three kids in three-and-a-half years. The first arrived when I was 22.

MARGARET That was a handful?

RENEE I remember at one point the four-month-old was in a cuddle seat on the floor, and I was tickling him with my foot while dealing with the other two. It was a handful and a footful.

MARGARET Were you a single mom?

RENEE By the time the oldest was almost four, the middle child one-and-a-half, and the youngest four months old, I was alone with them, until the youngest were 17 and 18 and they went to live with their dad for a while.

MARGARET How did you survive raising them by yourself?

RENEE Physically, I used to get very tired. Emotionally, I think I had a small, quiet nervous breakdown a few times a week. Financially, I was on welfare most of the time. For a brief period, I decided to be on the other side of the fence—I had had a lot of 'life' experience, my home felt like it was open in terms of the community, and the NDP was in power, rapidly making improvements to the system. I persuaded them to give me a job as a social worker. I did it for a couple of years until the Socreds got back in and started making the system bad again. Also, there were always crises within my case-load, heavy-duty problems to deal with, with people calling me at home about emergencies. I'd race home from work—which could mean a prison, a hospital, a foster home—pick up the kids from after-school care, make dinner, and muster up as much energy as I could manage, to be with them, totally, because I hadn't seen them all day. And they'd be pretty tired, too. If one of them got sick, often I couldn't stay home, but had to rely on a friend to keep them at their house. That felt terrible, that I couldn't be with them when they needed me. I thought, If I keep this routine up, my kids will end up needing a social worker. So, after two years, I quit and got a part-time job, with a group of artists, on a grant, helping to build an adventure playground at my kids' school. After that, I went back on welfare.

MARGARET You wanted to be with your kids?

RENEE Absolutely. They were my gift—and at times, my cross to bear. But they were my life, and I wanted very much to raise them, no matter what. I had made that commitment. And they often made me happy, gave me great joy.

MARGARET For you, that meant entering the welfare system? It dictated your structure. You had to do the welfare dance?

RENEE I didn't have much interference from them, although I was very aware that they were supporting me. Aside from the horribly small amount of money, there was not much interference, partly because I knew the system well enough to be able to use it as much as I could. It didn't intimidate me. But, at a certain point, the kids resented it.

MARGARET At school?

RENEE By the time they were pre-teens—although the school they went to was sort of 'alternate' and full of single-parent families without much money. I was very careful not to let them feel 'poor' and I wasn't very public about being on welfare, but they'd absorbed the social stigma attached. They would say things like, 'Ha, you have a university degree and look at you. Why should we go to school? Look what you've become.'

I would explain to them that welfare is just like any other money given out—whether it's Canada Council grants, unemployment insurance, tax breaks for big corporations. It's all the same money, and it's ours. Government money is money we've all paid in to, in one way or another. People needing financial help to raise kids should get it without any stigma attached to it. Parents who have the resources to do a good job are making an enormous contribution to society. We're a good investment, very productive, and it's financially the cheapest way to raise kids, who are in turn going to contribute to society.

MARGARET As compared to daycare?

RENEE I don't think one cancels out the other. Daycare is very important. I used daycare from the time my first kid was about three or four years old. Not from the minute it opened to the minute it closed, but as much as possible. I was lucky to find good daycare for them. No other adults had any regular contact with my kids except for the daycare people. I thought it very important for the kids to be exposed to 'uninvolved adults' who shared the same child-rearing philosophy I did.

MARGARET Extended family?

RENEE No. One day I had a partner bringing some money in, the next day I didn't. There was no money, no rent. I didn't drive. It was a very difficult situation—not that it had been easy before—but suddenly it became entirely up to me to deal with these three kids in every way. Once a week someone from Welfare came in and gave me a break in the afternoon—just baby-sat the kids, and I would go out for a few hours—which made me quite heady, I tell you.

MARGARET What did you do?

RENEE Sometimes I would just sit and have coffee by myself. Having some time alone was so important to me, because I never seemed to have any until late at night, at which point I was so tired that I would force myself to stay up and read or do something so that I could experience being awake and alone, because

I felt that sleep was almost a wasted activity—although I would always make sure I got enough sleep. I needed just a little bit of time to feel that I was alone.

MARGARET Other needs?

RENEE I had very few at that point. I really couldn't afford to have needs—although I always had friends, and I would see them when I could, but I couldn't go out very much. It was hard to find baby-sitters, because I didn't know too many people who were into baby-sitting. Most of my friends did not have children, and the few that did had only one. I never felt that there was an equal trade-off, that I could take their one kid and they, my three kids. I couldn't afford baby-sitters very often. If I did have a baby-sitter, then I could rarely afford to go to a movie, or whatever.

MARGARET Were there others in the same situation?

RENEE I knew very few, although I would do it differently now. I felt then, that if I had any real help, I would collapse. It was so important to keep everything together, and I felt so overwhelmed by the situation, I was worried that real help would make me crumble in a certain way, that I would never be able to get myself together again to be the kind of mother I wanted to be. I was very wary of becoming friends with people, because I felt that it wouldn't be a genuine relationship, you know, that it would be based on other factors.

I didn't avoid people who had kids, but I didn't go out of my way to look for them. Most of my friends were and still are artists without kids, and those were the people I wanted to remain in contact with, which seems bizarre now. I should have been saner and healthier. I just didn't have the resources to make that kind of change. Since I was in this almost impossible situation, I was going to do it as well as I could.

MARGARET It was difficult to accept help because your needs made you feel too vulnerable?

RENEE That's right. That's the word I was looking for. There was not a lot of support for women at home with kids, although I think the Women's Movement has dealt with that. It wasn't as though I was always saying no to people—there were not many people offering, partly because I didn't elicit or solicit it, and partly because I made sure to put on a very good front, because it was so important for people to see that I was not struggling, even though I was.

MARGARET Why was that important?

RENEE Because I felt that I had helped created the situation and, therefore, I was responsible for it, and nobody else was.

MARGARET This was the early seventies?

RENEE By the time I was alone with the kids, it was early '72.

MARGARET The focus was on getting women into the marketplace and not questioning the family unit as much. That came much later. No consciousness of children.

RENEE There were people in my life who were willing, if they had a relationship with me, to take on the kids. But, it was a package deal. If I didn't want the involvement, I wasn't going to get the support. Occasionally I thought, Maybe I should get involved in this relationship, it'd be good for the kids—but I never wanted to badly enough.

MARGARET So you put your own needs on hold?

RENEE Emotionally, I just wasn't ready to be with anyone, I wasn't ready to tap into my needs. There were some good people around, but I couldn't deal with them in any complex way.

MARGARET Did you read, talk to others? What oracles did you use?

RENEE I read Spock when they were very young, because they would wake up at two or three in the morning, and I would be up then, and Spock always seemed to have something in there that said, 'Don't worry, this has happened before, and it will happen again, and it is normal!' Concrete advice. The only book on parental training that I read was *P.E.T. (Parental Effectiveness Training)*, and I very rarely smacked my kids, but I once took that book and whacked one of the kids on the behind with it. Otherwise, I found it useless, just impossible. It wasn't concrete enough. Also, I wasn't just dealing with one kid, but also the interactions among three kids and me. More than anything, I was trying to be equitable and to encourage them to have respect for each other, for me, and for the world around them. [*joking*] What I wanted was for them to be good socialists and creative—that's not too much to ask for, is it?

MARGARET Why do women of our generation have little confidence in mothering?

RENEE Partly because, on the one hand, in our society mothering is considered important and valuable, and on the other, it's considered non-work, natural, nothing-to-it. Except when something goes wrong, and then the entire responsibility and blame is usually laid on the mother. Some 'adults' never get past that point. Also, our mothers were generally raised in very repressive times for women—lived depressed, frustrated lives, because all they were supposed to want was to be happy as wives and mothers, with little support to fulfil themselves in other ways. We're reaping the benefits of feminism.

But, when we become mothers, often under stress, we revert back to sometimes very painful periods of our lives as children. Old memories and patterns of behaviour come charging through, except we're on the reverse end of it now. Mistakes our parents made and we were so anxious not to repeat, we do repeat, because of sheer conditioning. I don't think it's preventable because it's internalized, unconscious, but when it happens we can try to be aware of it and work it out. Having the opportunity to 're-do' it is one of the perks of parenting. I think I owed it to my kids to be as honest as possible with them, to let them see that I'm a person, too, and the product of my own upbringing.

MARGARET Two different attitudes around children, then, controlling or permissive?

RENEE Single parents feel particularly vulnerable because we don't share the responsibility for raising the kids and we are incredibly aware of the influence we have on our children. Luckily, kids are born with lungs, and cry, and make us stop thinking so much and just react to their needs, instead. Because if we sat back and intellectualized the right move, we would be paralysed by fear. It is very difficult to find security, but it is important, if we love these kids, and if we remember how we were as kids, and if we have any common sense—then it will be alright. It's an interaction. It's not just us doing it to the kids, it's the kids relating back to us. We have to trust it.

Dropping Out In Mexico
Rebel Mother, Rebel Grandmother

Sidney Shadbolt, born in 1921 in Vancouver, B.C.
Mother of David, Jamie, and Kate
Interviewed by Margaret Dragu

MARGARET The first question I ask everybody is, 'When did you first want to have a baby?'

SIDNEY I never wanted to have a baby.

MARGARET When did you first find out that you were going to have a baby?

SIDNEY When I was pregnant, naturally.

MARGARET How old were you?

SIDNEY I was about 21, 22.

MARGARET Were you married?

SIDNEY Yes.

MARGARET And when you found out you were pregnant, you said—

SIDNEY Oh, I didn't say or think anything about it, because that's what you did in those days. You got married and you got pregnant—if you didn't you were a freak. I didn't know anybody who didn't get pregnant after they got married. I had no great wishes to have a baby or to be pregnant. It was just something that you did.

MARGARET Can you remember how you felt when you found out you were actually pregnant? Disappointed, happy, elated, shocked?

SIDNEY No, no, I wasn't disappointed, and I wasn't shocked. I just thought, Well, this is the next stage of my life.

MARGARET At 21 or so?

SIDNEY Oh, I might have been 22. It was during the war.

MARGARET And your husband, he wasn't going to fight in the war, he was going to be around? Did you know? Or did you think you were all going to—

SIDNEY No, he wasn't going off to war, because he was in a job that required him to stay. There were some people, depending on their job, who had to stay. They could not go off to war, even if they wanted to. There was no question of him going away, or of trying to have a baby because he might go off to war, and he might get killed, and this would be the sentimental link.

MARGARET So you found yourself pregnant, and where were you living at the time?

SIDNEY I was living in Winnipeg.

MARGARET Did you have family around you? Was your mother around?

SIDNEY I had my mother and my father and my brothers. One of my brothers was probably away by then. They went back and forth. And my grandmother and my grandfather and my aunts.

MARGARET So there were women around you who were thrilled that you were going to have a baby.

SIDNEY Oh, god, yes.

MARGARET You had that supportive family push.

SIDNEY Yes. My mother was just, oh, just thrilled. Way more than I was. It was quite funny actually, to see mother sort of twitting around.

MARGARET How did that make you feel, that they were so excited and you weren't necessarily?

SIDNEY I just thought it was a big fuss about somebody being pregnant. Everybody got pregnant, didn't they? Everybody that I knew did.

MARGARET Did you have any ideas about how you wanted to have the baby? In a hospital? Did you want to do something different than they did, or did you accept that you were going to do what they did? Or were there any options?

SIDNEY There weren't any options

MARGARET People weren't running off and having babies underneath waterfalls and stuff like that.

SIDNEY No, I never even read about anybody doing that. Oh, that would have been far out.

MARGARET Had it in the hospital?

SIDNEY Oh, absolutely.

MARGARET Family doctor, family hospital. There weren't many options.

SIDNEY No, you didn't have a a family doctor, you went to an obstetrician. And you went to a hospital. In fact, I don't think there were midwives in those days. There must have been.

MARGARET But not in Winnipeg.

SIDNEY Not that I ever heard of. I wasn't encouraged to even know about stuff like that.

MARGARET So you did that then? Went off to a hospital? And the first baby was a boy?

SIDNEY Yes. I went off to the hospital, and in those days you stayed nine days. Can you imagine? Nine days. They treated you like an invalid.

MARGARET Did you feel like an invalid?

SIDNEY No.

MARGARET You wanted to go home. You were 21 and young...

SIDNEY You can do what you want after 21, right?

MARGARET When you went home with the baby, were you surprised? Did you find any shock of responsibility for taking care of the baby?

SIDNEY No, because I didn't have to take care of it.

MARGARET What happened?

SIDNEY I had a nurse, because that's something that people did. They had a nurse that came back with them. I think they were called practical nurses. I had a practical nurse. Her name was Miss Johnson. She was a dragon. Oh god, she was a dragon. I was scared to death of her, but she was very nice with the baby. She was terrific. She was someone that other people I knew had had. She looked after the baby until the mother got back on her feet. Of course, the mother was never going to get back on her feet as long as she had a nurse.

MARGARET How long did Miss Johnson stay?

SIDNEY She stayed about 10 days.

MARGARET Why was she a dragon? Not a dragon with the baby, she was a dragon with you?

SIDNEY Well, she was a 'Miss,' for one thing.

MARGARET *Miss* Johnson.

SIDNEY She was *Miss* Johnson. I don't even know what her first name was.

MARGARET Not roaringly intimate.

SIDNEY Oh, god, no. She made it very clear that *she* was looking after the baby, and that she had her ways. That I, being a mere first-timer, knew nothing. Which was quite right. I knew nothing. I think she even made the dinner. She stayed overnight. She was there. Then she went on to somebody else.

MARGARET How did you feel when she'd left?

SIDNEY I thought, Omigod, now I have to bath this baby. I have to do everything. I can remember the first few nights, I slept in the nursery. We had what she called a nursery. All the baby's things were there. A changing table, and a chest of drawers, and a bed as well. The first night, I slept in there because I thought, Surely this kid will die. It didn't seem right to leave the baby in a room by itself. It turned out that the baby was quite fine by itself. That was the only time I ever did that.

MARGARET Did you find that you agreed with what Miss Johnson had set up? Or, when you were looking at what she was doing, did you think, Oh, I would never do that!

SIDNEY There were a lot of things. I thought, She'll only be here for 10 days, and then I'll do it my way after that.

MARGARET Can you remember anything that you felt was different that you wanted to do, than what she did?

SIDNEY It was quite funny, actually. She had a quite mistaken theory that a baby's bowels always moved after he'd eaten, and she used to hold this poor little baby over a pottie—

MARGARET A week-old baby?

SIDNEY : Oh, yes. I thought, Oh well, it's nothing to do with me, even though it's my baby. She'll be here for 10 days or so, and then I will just stick the diapers on the child like everybody else does. I was quite glad actually when she left.

MARGARET Sounds like it. Dragon lady seems appropriate. Sounds a bit Victorian.

SIDNEY Oh, very. She was very efficient and very nice with the baby. Very comfortable, and very much at ease, and handled the baby very well. Way better than I did, because I didn't know.

Didn't take long though.

MARGARET It takes practice.

SIDNEY It wasn't my baby.

MARGARET It wasn't your baby until she left.

SIDNEY No, not at all.

MARGARET I can imagine. That seems fairly intimidating.

SIDNEY Oh, it was.

MARGARET Extra hands are nice to have around. That's why I asked about family members. As long as you get along with them.

SIDNEY We all got along fine.

MARGARET But the nurse seems like a foreign element. Certainly old-school.

SIDNEY Oh, very. Very old-school. Even in my day that was old-school.

MARGARET So when she was gone you were on your own, and you put diapers on and figured out, Well, surely I can bath this baby.

SIDNEY The baby didn't die. Nothing terrible happened.

MARGARET And you get better at it. It's one of those things that you just keep doing.

SIDNEY Oh, sure. In a week I felt fine.

MARGARET Were you depressed afterwards? Did you have baby blues or anything? Can you remember?

SIDNEY No, not at all. No. Why would you?

MARGARET Well, some people do.

SIDNEY I could never understand that.

MARGARET You never did with any of the kids?

SIDNEY No.

MARGARET How old was David when you found out you were pregnant for the second time?

SIDNEY I lived in Winnipeg when he was born, and then we moved to a little town in Quebec, a French town.

MARGARET Did you learn to speak French?

SIDNEY Oh, of course. Well, a kind of French. Kitchen French. Let's see now ... David was two years old.

MARGARET Was that a shock, having two?

SIDNEY No.

MARGARET No?

SIDNEY No. I lived in a little village, and there was no hospital. This was outside of Montreal. I went into the hospital in Montreal. The Royal Victoria, I think it is. Just went on the bus to get my check-ups. When it came time to have the baby, I think they decided that, because I lived so far away and there were no taxis—this was a very traditional French village, and they didn't even like the English people who lived there. There was a store there, and they wouldn't sell us anything. It was hard.

MARGARET You had to bring in food from Montreal?

SIDNEY No, a grocer from another village used to come a couple of times a week to find out what people wanted, and then he'd come back the next day. There were no taxis—they decided that I should go into hospital ahead of time. Which I did.

MARGARET And wait? Or they were going to induce?

SIDNEY No, I had to wait for a certain amount of time, and if nothing happened, they would induce the labour.

MARGARET Who took care of the first boy, David, while you were—

SIDNEY The people next door, who had 10 children. They also had boarders. They were night-shift people.

MARGARET So one more two-year-old wasn't much of a problem.

SIDNEY No problem at all. In fact, we took his bed over, and I'd never bothered to hem the sheets. This woman was so shocked.

MARGARET With 10 kids, she was still hemming sheets?

SIDNEY Can you imagine? They were an obsession with her. The guy was a labourer in the plant that my husband ran, the war plant. She just came over one day and said, 'What are you gonna do when your baby's born?'

MARGARET Good question.

SIDNEY Very good question. I said, 'I'll just find somebody in the village.' And she said, 'Well, he can come over here.'

MARGARET Great. And she did it out of the goodness of her heart? She didn't expect to be paid?

SIDNEY Oh, no!

MARGARET You were neighbours. That's great. So, you went, and you waited, and it came.

SIDNEY I waited, and they finally did induce the labour, and Jamie was born. It was very quick.

MARGARET The second one is. Sometimes, anyway.

SIDNEY Apparently, but it was really interesting. While I was in there, there was a woman down the hall who had just had her eighth child, and she refused to take it home. Just refused. She was quite a wealthy woman. She was married to a doctor. I remember I used to talk to her, and I said, 'Is it really true that you're not taking your baby home?' She said, 'Look, I've already got eight children. I do *not* want this child, and I am *not* taking it home.' I said, 'Oh, you'll change your mind when it comes time to leave.' She said, 'No, I won't.' And she didn't. She left it. That was that. She said that there were lots of people in the world who would like to have the baby. Healthy, good genes, good-background baby. She said, 'I've got eight kids. Why would I want another one?'

MARGARET How did that make you feel?

SIDNEY Oh, I was scandalized, but full of admiration, too. That this woman would, in those days, defy the hospital rules. The rules at the hospital at the time were that you had to take your child home. It didn't matter how sick you were, or how poor you were, or what terrible care that kid might get. You had to take it home. She just refused. How she got away with it, I don't know.

MARGARET It obviously stuck in your mind, made a real impression.

SIDNEY It wasn't as if she were a loony woman, or schizzy.

MARGARET Or being beaten, or very poor.

SIDNEY No. She was a perfectly nice woman, and a perfectly nice husband, and the kids used to come. She had lots of money. It wasn't as if she couldn't look after the baby. I just thought, Oh my—and the woman in the bed next to me, that was the best part. She was a French-Canadian woman who had been trying to have a baby for many years, but she couldn't feed the baby.

MARGARET She couldn't breast-feed.

SIDNEY She was so disappointed and so uptight. I said, 'What's the big deal? As long as the kid's healthy. You're just getting yourself into a sweat.' She was, too, she was in a sweat the whole time. She thought that this woman who didn't take her baby was just a murderer. An absolute murderer.

MARGARET People have very strong, *strong* feelings about motherhood.

SIDNEY Oh, god, yes.

MARGARET On the one hand it's sentimental, and on the other hand very rigid. Today, too. It's no different.

SIDNEY This woman was very sentimental, but at the same time, she'd been brought up in the forties—it's hard for young women nowadays, to imagine what it was like in those days.

MARGARET How few options there were. Very little birth control. Birth control pills weren't even invented. There were very few methods of birth control.

SIDNEY Oh, god, no. You couldn't even get a diaphragm, unless you were married. There were no options.

MARGARET And abortion was an incredible sin.

SIDNEY Abortion! In Quebec? God no. Listen, where I lived in Quebec, you couldn't even go out on your bicycle in a pair of shorts. I did, and I used to get into trouble from the priest all the time. He was always visiting me.

MARGARET Telling you not to? Because it was sinful, or because you were inciting men?

SIDNEY I had no idea. I said to him one time, 'I don't understand why I can't go around in my shorts on my bike. Because,' I said, 'you see those girls in the village ...' At that time there were something called dirndl skirts.

MARGARET Drop-waisted sort of things?

SIDNEY No. But they were very full. When the wind blew, it would blow them over their heads. I said, 'Now half those girls don't even wear knickers—so now, tell me why I can't wear shorts.' He didn't even have an answer.

MARGARET It's interesting—I get a sense you were interested in defying authority from that early time.

SIDNEY No, not really.

MARGARET In some ways. You said that to a priest, and you had an inkling about Miss Johnson. You were preparing for later adventures, and we shall get to those. Now, you had two children, and you hadn't necessarily planned the second one, but you assumed that you would have more than one, that you would have two or three children, probably.

SIDNEY I never even thought about it.

MARGARET So you didn't use birth control?

SIDNEY Oh, I did, but it doesn't always work.

MARGARET No, that's true. That's the notorious thing with birth control.

SIDNEY It just all happened.

MARGARET And you accepted it.

SIDNEY That was what you did.

MARGARET How old was Jamie when you were pregnant with your third child, Kate?

SIDNEY Let's see, there's 18 months difference between them. Not even 18 months, 15. A year and a half.

MARGARET That's quite a handful.

SIDNEY Oh, I know.

MARGARET Were you still in Northern Quebec when Kate came, or had you moved?

SIDNEY The war finished, and my husband got a job in Victoria, British Columbia. So we moved.

MARGARET Kate was born in Victoria in a hospital?

SIDNEY Yes, at Jubilee hospital.

MARGARET Then you had three kids at home. Were there family, relatives around? His family, your family, both?

SIDNEY My parents had moved out to British Columbia and lived in Sydney, so my mother was around.

MARGARET And did they baby-sit? Did you have baby-sitters? Did you pay for baby-sitters?

SIDNEY I had somebody—Mrs. Powell, I think it was—who used to come, and I don't know what she did. She looked after the kids and cleaned the house. Mostly looked after them a couple of days a week, so that I could go and visit my mother, or I would go to the beach, or visit my friends.

MARGARET So, you'd have maybe two days off a week for yourself through Mrs. Powell.

SIDNEY Half a day at least. Powers, her name was. Mrs. Powers. She was really nice. She liked kids. Oh, she was great. She was terrific. She didn't have any kids. All my friends had kids, and we used to visit back and forth.

MARGARET Were there nursery schools or pre-schools? Or was it mostly people like Mrs. Powers? I'm curious about what sort of options you had, to get away from the kids.

SIDNEY Well, there were nursery schools—David went to a little nursery school—but not a lot of them. Most people looked after their own kids.

MARGARET How old were your children when you went to Mexico, and how did you decide on Mexico as a place to go?

SIDNEY I knew somebody who'd spent quite a bit of time in Mexico, and I'd always wanted to go there. In fact, before we actually went there, I went with a friend to Mexico, so I knew sort of what it was like. Though not to the place where we eventually lived. I found out that in this little place there were no malaria mosquitoes, and there was a school, a good school. Two good schools. There was a good doctor. The water supply was good. Nobody was going to get any terrible disease.

The reason I went was, I thought my kids had too many material things. They just expected to have bicycles and cameras, and to go to the best schools—which they did. They just had too much. It was as though what they read about in Social Science—which was what they called it then, I guess they still do—was a novel. It was something you read about. There were not people in the world that—

MARGARET Were starving—

SIDNEY There were not people in the world that didn't live the way they did. I thought, That's really terrible.

MARGARET It's interesting you decided on that. There was not a wave of people who were all interested in doing that. You weren't surrounded by people who had thought of it, and you absorbed it.

SIDNEY Oh, god, no.

MARGARET Can you imagine where that conviction came from, where that idea came from?

SIDNEY I don't know. I just knew that kids living in Victoria should know more about the world than what was in Victoria. I don't know if I would have felt like that if I'd lived in Montreal or in Toronto, but certainly, living in B.C.—it's so insulated, and people are so smug here, that—I didn't want my kids to turn out the way most British Columbians are—people who just seemed to me they'd never been anywhere, and they didn't want to go anywhere. They don't like the French, although they've never set foot in Quebec and never would.

MARGARET Did you say to your husband one day, 'I think my children, our children, really need to have a broader experience, and I'm going to take them down to Mexico.' Is that what you said over dinner one day?

SIDNEY I'm sure we talked it over, but I would have made my own decision.

MARGARET How old were the kids when you went down there?

SIDNEY Let's see, David was 13. Jamie must have been 11, and Kate must have been 10. Somewhere around there.

MARGARET So, off you went to Mexico.

SIDNEY I went with a friend. She didn't have any children.

MARGARET How was it when you got there? Certainly the Mexicans would have been surprised to see a woman with children with no husband, although there are widows. Did you pretend that you were a widow?

SIDNEY No. They were far too polite to make any comments.

MARGARET And you found a house?

SIDNEY We stayed in a hotel the first three days, and then we found a house. It was a house made out of mud-brick. It was very modest. There was no furniture in it. There was an outhouse. There was no electricity. There was no running water. Oh, there was electricity, for two hours at night.

MARGARET That's very Mexican. Just two hours at night.

SIDNEY It is. We lived in a little town of about 5,000 people.

MARGARET So, you set about going to market, and doing all the things to run a household. You learned Spanish.

SIDNEY I already knew how to speak Spanish. I'd studied it through correspondence, and I'd had teachers, too, and I'd taught the kids a little bit—a teeny bit.

MARGARET How was it adjusting? What was a typical day like once you got settled?

SIDNEY It was difficult to get food. There wasn't a market, contrary to what people think. Not in that town, anyway. There were little places. If you were a Mexican, you knew how to get stuff. We had a cook, Sabina, and she came every morning at 7:30 with whatever she could get to make breakfast. There was no milk. You had to get on a list if you wanted milk. We had canned milk. The kids would get up. They were so used to Sabina that they used to sit on their beds and let her dress them. She'd put their clothes on them and do their hair, and off they'd go to school with their school bags and their water bottles—because the water wasn't safe to drink. They'd drink the water on the way to school and after that they'd drink any old water. They were fine.

MARGARET As long as you didn't know.

SIDNEY As long as I didn't know. What can you do, anyway?

MARGARET Jim keeps saying, 'Being a parent is about loss of control, so just relax.'

SIDNEY Yeah, just relax. You're not going to know everything that they do anyhow, so why bother?

MARGARET So, they'd be off at school.

SIDNEY They'd be off at school, and then Sabina and I, and the woman that I was with, would decide what shopping had to be done for the day. Because you had to go out actively and look for food. You couldn't just go to the store. Sabina would do it. She knew where to get everything. And what would I do? Well, we'd just go off to the beach, and learn Spanish, more Spanish. That's what we did. Then at night, we used to help the kids. The kids did two school programs, the one at the school, the Mexican school, and another one from home.

MARGARET A kind of correspondence course?

SIDNEY It wasn't really correspondence. I just took their books and made them do stuff. You see, they thought they wouldn't be going to school there. They thought I was not serious. But the second day we were there I said, 'Okay—'

MARGARET Off to school. That's where the big social intercourse is going to happen for them, with those kids.

SIDNEY Exactly, and it didn't take long. In the evenings, we went to bed early, around 8:00 or 9:00. There was no electricity. Well, there was a lamp. We'd write letters. I can't remember what we did at night. People would come over.

MARGARET So, you got to know your neighbours.

SIDNEY Well, not the neighbours especially. Everybody lived behind a wall. The houses were all on a street. Next door to us was a little *frijole* place, where they made *frijoles*. No, not *frijoles*.

MARGARET A *tortilleria*? That machine ...

SIDNEY No, like this [*slapping hands rhythmically*]. That sound. That was the sound we used to hear every morning. I lived beside the local spot for beer and *tortilla*. The kids hung out there.

MARGARET Who then were the people who came to visit? Who did you get to know?

SIDNEY I got to know a man who played guitar. He used to come. He met the kids. There were a couple of wrestlers, a Mexican wrestler and a German wrestler. Various people we met on the beach would come around.

MARGARET They would come for dinner, or after dinner?

SIDNEY No, we never invited anybody for dinner. It was too difficult.

MARGARET And also, being two women alone, you didn't want to stir things up. Or was that a factor?

SIDNEY We stirred enough trouble up. It was enough.

MARGARET Did the priest come to visit?

SIDNEY No. I don't think I ever saw the priest.

MARGARET You weren't running around in shorts? You knew enough not to.

SIDNEY Oh, god, no. You could wear shorts on the beach.

MARGARET But you changed at the beach.

SIDNEY You wore a skirt over your shorts. The minute you got to the beach, then you took your skirt off. You could do anything you wanted on the beach.

MARGARET Did your children receive the part of their education that you wanted them to receive? The living education, not the schooling?

SIDNEY Yes, it was a success. And the education was a success too, because they were way ahead in science and in mathematics.

MARGARET From the Mexican school?

SIDNEY From the little village school. It was extraordinary. It was not a Church school, because it's separate in Mexico.

MARGARET I've seen those *escuelas* with the little girls in their little uniforms. They love their teachers. They would kiss their teachers before they went home for lunch. They loved it. Great schools.

SIDNEY Yes, Kate loved it. The little girls used to sit around in a courtyard. Beautiful school that the girls went to. The girls went to one school and the boys another. Absolutely beautiful school, with birdcages and wonderful plants. It was quite a modern building, and all the schoolrooms opened onto a patio. The little girls would sit around doing cross-stitch at certain times of the day, and the teachers would be reading to them. It was lovely. The boys' school was quite different. It was very vicious and violent.

MARGARET They didn't like their school as much?

SIDNEY Oh, they did. They could brawl. They could fight like the rest of them.

MARGARET They liked it all round? You were happy there, all of you?

SIDNEY We were.

MARGARET How long did you stay?

SIDNEY A year? A school year.

MARGARET Then you decided that that was enough?

SIDNEY No, then I went back again with Kate.

MARGARET You went back to Victoria and the boys stayed.

SIDNEY You could only stay in Mexico for six months, and then you had to renew your visa, unless you wanted to bribe somebody. I can remember one night the police coming, saying, 'You have to come right down to the hotel now, because we want to check your passports.' I said, 'Well, I won't.' They said, 'But you have to. We're the police.' I said, 'I don't care. I know perfectly well my passport is fully in order, and I know perfectly well that you'll be there tomorrow. I'll be there at 11 in the morning. See you then.' Closed the door. I mean, they're just looking for a party. Not that they would have hurt you, but I didn't see why ... and, sure enough, our passports were in perfect order.

MARGARET Why did you decide that the boys would stay, and you and Kate would go back?

SIDNEY Well, because I had a lover by then.

MARGARET Ah! In Mexico?

SIDNEY Yes, in this town.

MARGARET Oh! You weren't going to bed every night at eight o'clock with the children! But why did the boys not come? You felt it was too much to handle? Or they were getting too old?

SIDNEY They just became boarders at their school in Victoria instead of day-boys. So, that was all right. But they hated it.

MARGARET Did you feel guilty?

SIDNEY Ah, a bit. A little bit, but I figured a lot worse things were going to happen to them than boarding school.

MARGARET Than not having their mother there every night while they're asleep.

SIDNEY No. No. My family tried to make me feel guilty. My mother especially.

MARGARET What did they say?

SIDNEY Oh, it was dreadful. To go to Mexico in the first place. Dreadful. Take your children off to a foreign country? God knows what they might get.

MARGARET Germs. Ideas.

SIDNEY Germs, yes. She never thought about ideas. How could they possibly get any ideas?

MARGARET They're only children. But to go a second time and leave your sons was very bad.

SIDNEY Very suspect.

MARGARET We do have the idea that mothers are martyrs, and anything less than martyrdom is extremely wicked.

SIDNEY I don't think my mother was into being a martyr, but she was into doing what was proper for those days—I think we've said 'those days' at least 10 times now.

MARGARET Those days ...

SIDNEY In those days ...

MARGARET But was it something about boarding school, or you possibly having your own life, or your own ideas, or your own fun, or your own sense of self, that was it?

SIDNEY You just didn't go away and leave your children. Nobody. You just didn't do that.

MARGARET But there were boarding schools. There were other boys in boarding school besides your two sons.

SIDNEY Yes, but just to be so frivolous to go off to Mexico. It was somehow not ... I don't think they minded so much. My father didn't give a damn. I don't think it was that time. I think it was when we first went. I'd been in Mexico before then and left my kids at home.

MARGARET With them. With your mother.

SIDNEY No, I never left my kids with my mother. Only my animals.

MARGARET Only your animals! When you went to Mexico the first time, who did you leave the children with?

SIDNEY I left them with my husband, and we had a housekeeper. That worked perfectly. They were in school all day.

MARGARET It's interesting that you did have such different ideas about being a mother than your mother did, without knowing a direct example. It's not that you saw a girlfriend do this, or a community—and you stood up to the cops in Mexico, and that's also very ... individual.

SIDNEY Speaking of standing up to the cops, there was another time when one of my kids ended up in jail. Do you want to know about that?

MARGARET Sure.

SIDNEY All part of being a mother.

MARGARET You bet. They do things when you're not looking that are out of your control. How old was he?

SIDNEY It was when David was 13. There was a big rivalry in the town with the kids about the wrestlers, the Mexican wrestler and the German wrestler. These two men were in the town prior to their fight in the match. The kids got to know them. All the kids did, and they'd start making wagers about who was going to win, you see. Of course all the Mexican kids were for the Mexican, and my kids were for Karl, the German fellow. The day came for the wrestling, and I was not the least bit interested in the wrestling—but, unknown to me, David had a knife, which I had forbidden him to have.

He bought it in a market on the way down. We were on a bus at one point, and we were in a little town, and he'd bought a knife. Then, with his extra *pesos*, he'd had the knife sharpened. I said, 'David, you cannot have that knife. Now just get rid of it.' But then I didn't check. The day of the wrestling match came, and I was on the beach. This was on a Sunday afternoon. Somebody came running down to the beach and said, 'Oh, you'd better come. There's been a little accident, and your son's in jail.' I thought, Oh, god. I found out that there'd been an argument about these two wrestlers, and David had pulled a knife out of his pocket. Out of a sheath. It was around his waist at that point. As he pulled it out, he grazed the arm of a little girl.

Well, every kid was gone—something I found out later from my friend Dyllis Poole, is that in South America and in Mexico, it's okay if you don't get caught. In order not to get caught, you just run. My kids didn't know that. You stuck around to see what would happen, to take the consequences, and also to explain it. David didn't do it deliberately—it was an accident.

Anyway, he was hauled off to jail, and I found out that, if I paid, I could get him out of jail. It was the Chief of Police who I was talking to. He said, 'Well, you just pay me.' I said, 'What for?' And he said, 'To get your child out of jail. You don't want him there overnight, do you?' I said, 'What's wrong with jail?' He said, 'Nothing.' 'When would he be getting out?' 'Tomorrow. Unless you pay me.' I said, 'I'm not paying you. That's bribery. Why should I pay you to get the kid out of jail? He's in there for a good reason.' He was a bit surprised. So, David just stayed there overnight. The next day he was let out.

MARGARET What did David say? Did he tell you what happened in jail?

SIDNEY He said he'd found out that they don't feed you in jail. Why didn't I come like the Mexicans' families and feed him? I said, 'I don't know. It didn't hurt you for the night to be without food,' and I said, 'Don't they feed them in jail?' He said, 'No. Families bring food and pass it through.'

MARGARET What did you do? Did you sleep that night? Did you worry about him endlessly?

SIDNEY No, when you're young, you don't worry too much. Why would I worry? He was safe in jail. He couldn't get out, what was there to worry about?

MARGARET Oh, assault.

SIDNEY I never thought of that. If I had thought about it, omigod. Never thought of it! Well, he was just a kid. Why would they ...? They wouldn't assault a kid. Not in those days.

MARGARET In these days, orphanages and jails seem to be extremely dangerous places. Particularly the orphanages.

SIDNEY In these days, I would have paid to get him out. But not then. This was in the fifties.

MARGARET And he wasn't hurt?

SIDNEY I don't think even his pride was hurt. He knew he shouldn't have had that knife. I said, 'What did you do with the knife?' He said, 'I left it there.' I said, 'Good. Good thinking.'

MARGARET You have a very loving but unsentimental view of motherhood. I've seen you with the red-haired daughter of your friend—and you were very clear with her. Not parental, but nearly parental. You were very clear about logical consequences. You said, 'If this, then that. If you do this, then you do that. If you don't do this, then you lose this privilege.' That seemed very clear. Is that how you raised your own children, with that idea of 'if this, then that'?

SIDNEY I just always thought and taught them that they were responsible for their own actions. If they did something stupid, there were consequences to that. They had to live with those consequences. Maybe it's because I was brought up in a very protected way.

MARGARET What do you mean by protected?

SIDNEY We never went to other kids' places overnight. Money was never talked about in the house. My mother was very careful about what kids we played with. They had to know what families they came from. That sort of thing.

MARGARET You must have found that confining. Does that play into why you took your kids to Mexico? You wanted them to have more real life?

SIDNEY Yes, I only knew certain kinds of kids, you see. The school that I went to was not an ordinary school. There wasn't a big variety of kids. In fact, where we lived in Winnipeg, I never saw a Black person, except people who worked on the trains. There were no Chinese people at any school I ever went to. There was nobody, except what we were, because we lived in that neighbourhood. Now, if we'd lived in the North End of Winnipeg, we still wouldn't have seen any. You might have seen the odd Chinese person, but in those days Chinese people did not come and live in Winnipeg. There were a few Chinese restaurants, and my father knew Chinese through his business, but they were all people who ran stores. Or the Black people worked in the railway.

MARGARET No wonder there's this entrenched fear of others. Because of our history. We were so separate.

SIDNEY Absolutely, and it wasn't until after the war that there was an influx of people into Canada. I used to talk to my mother about the way she was brought up. It was just dreadful. She wasn't going to bring her children up like that.

MARGARET How was she raised?

SIDNEY It was during the First World War, in a small town in Manitoba, Portage-au-Prairie, which was intended to be the centre of Manitoba, but it didn't happen. Everybody from Portage moved to Winnipeg.

MARGARET What did she dislike about how she was raised?

SIDNEY Nothing, except that it was a small place, and they weren't allowed to do anything. Her class 'didn't do that.' When the war came, my mother wanted to become a nurse and go overseas. Her father, my grandfather, said, 'If you do that, my dear, you needn't bother coming back, and we certainly will not support you.' But she did it.

MARGARET Anyway.

SIDNEY Anyway. And my grandmother's father was the Lieutenant-Governor of Prince Edward Island. All the people that they knew were Liberals and Protestants.

MARGARET Narrows it down even farther.

SIDNEY Even more than that. And, of course, in those ...

MARGARET In those days.

SIDNEY You can call this tape 'In Those Days.' The girls didn't go to school. They were sent away to school. If you were a Protestant and a Conservative, you didn't speak. If you were a Catholic and a—

MARGARET Liberal.

SIDNEY You didn't speak. When my grandmother got married, and lived in various places, like Winnipeg, she used to go to the races. She was a gambler.

MARGARET Ooh!

SIDNEY Quite a good gambler. She used to play mahjong—for money.

MARGARET But, she was still operating within very strong confines.

SIDNEY She had to.

MARGARET But you were all kind of itching to get out.

SIDNEY Don't you think most people are?

MARGARET I guess you're right.

SIDNEY I bet you if you started talking to people, you'd find that they mostly all are.

MARGARET Well, I'm really curious about your relationship with your kids now. I get a sense—although I can't tell—that being a mother never stops. Even if you don't see them all the time. Is that true? Of course you see Kate, and you see Jamie. And now there are grandchildren.

SIDNEY Oh, you can never get rid of your kids. You can get rid of your husband, your animals, your friends—well, not if they're really friends. You can get rid of your animals and your husband. You can never get rid of your kids. You might as well be on good terms with them.

MARGARET Great advice.

SIDNEY It's ridiculous that people can't get along with their family. It's silly. As long as you can keep a dialogue going no matter what happens—some of my kids did some pretty awful things. One of them freaked out completely on drugs for three years. Heavy, heavy, heavy, heavy drugs. In isolation for a long time, and darkness, but we always kept in contact. Whereas I know a lot of parents where, if there's any hint of drugs, they just don't speak to them.

MARGARET They pull the plug.

SIDNEY I think that, if you're civilized, you can get along with your family.

MARGARET But you can keep talking vaguely, and not really have any intimacy.

SIDNEY Yes.

MARGARET That's not what you're talking about, is it?

SIDNEY No. I'm not talking about that. I'm talking about support. I can remember when I was a kid, we used to play hookey from school sometimes. I didn't. I was too scared to, but my brothers did. I was in the same room at one point as my brother. We'd start off to school together ...

MARGARET You'd get there. He wouldn't.

SIDNEY Yes, and then I'd be asked, and it was very hard. I said to my mother, 'What am I supposed to do?' She said, 'Well, you just have to tell that he started off with you, and you don't know what happened.' But she said, 'You know, you always stick up for your family no matter what happens.' You stick up for your family. You don't put your family down.

MARGARET How do you keep that intimacy if you disapprove of each other? For instance, when you'd done something when you were raising your children, and they didn't approve. They didn't stop seeing you, I take it.

SIDNEY No, they didn't, but when I don't agree with one of my kids—especially Kate, Kate is very confrontational—I just say, 'Well, Kate, not everybody has that view.' When they were kids, little kids, they'd want to know what was right. I would say, 'Some people think this is right, and other people think that is right. You have to decide for yourselves what is right. You can't think what I think.'

MARGARET But it's hard not to judge, if you love someone, and you're close to them, and they're doing something you think is crazy, or harmful, or just silly, even—it doesn't have to be that big.

SIDNEY You can say that you think they're a damn fool, and they need a kick in the head.

MARGARET But you say it in an intimate way, and you keep on talking. It seems you've maintained the dialogue. I'm sure you can't even imagine the estrangement most families have, where they just don't know each other at all.

SIDNEY You just shut up. I've found that, as you get older—when you get to be as old as I am, Margaret, you get to be extremely tolerant. I have a friend who's a teacher in Ontario in a French school. Oh, god, the stuff she puts up with at that school, and the things that go on. I say, 'God, Pat, you're really tolerant.' She says, 'I'm not tolerant. I'm just indifferent to most of it.' She says, 'There's a big difference between tolerance and indifference.' There's some stuff that I am completely indifferent to. If they want to do that, fine. It's not my business.

MARGARET You do seem very intimate with Kate and Jamie.

SIDNEY Oh, we're good friends.

MARGARET And how do you like being a grandmother?

SIDNEY I'm not very good at it.

MARGARET Why?

SIDNEY I don't have pictures, and I don't talk about them all the time. They're okay. I'm not—

MARGARET You're not an active grandma.

SIDNEY They're alright once they get to be eight, or nine, or 10. But when they're two or three—

MARGARET Oh, they're definitely a handful. You don't miss being close to them?

SIDNEY No, god. No, they live in Victoria. The latest one.

MARGARET You're probably a perfect grandmother. You're just not like the movies grandmothers.

SIDNEY Amos is a terrific kid. I like him. We get along just fine. I don't know about Stick. I'm sure we'll get along. He's just a little kid, now, and I can't be bothered. He doesn't live here. If they lived here, it would be different. But I'm not a hands-on grandmother. I don't kiss them, and have fits over them.

MARGARET There's a great forgiveness in that separation between generations. Grandparent and grandchild.

SIDNEY I got along well with my grandparents. They were a bit zizzy. My grandparents were not like other people's grandparents. They weren't fat and cuddly, didn't wear housedresses with aprons. My grandmother was very zizzy—always on the go—and she used to take us to movies. She used to come to the lake sometimes when my mother had to go away somewhere. My cousins lived with us. We used to take our clothes off, and go in the water at night.

MARGARET How did being a mother change your life? Or did you start young enough that maybe it didn't matter?

SIDNEY You've got to be kidding to ask a question like that. Come on, Margaret, get real!

MARGARET Can you answer in 10 words or less? Could you?

SIDNEY How has it affected my life? If I weren't a mother, I'd be a lawyer. I'd have lots of money. I'd have different kinds of friends. I'd have fabulous clothes.

MARGARET Doesn't sound so bad, does it?

SIDNEY Doesn't sound bad at all! I'd have lots of lovers. I wouldn't have to give a damn what people thought—but when you have kids, they expect a certain level of behaviour. Well, not behaviour. Certain standards.

MARGARET A certain amount of love and security.

SIDNEY Oh, that's given, but I can remember Kate saying, 'Remember when you said so-and-so?' I'd say, 'No.' And she'd say, 'Well, I remember that. I know there are certain things you just don't do. I remember you telling us that.' Well, I don't remember that. And the boys have said that, too. When you think back, you think, They never learned a damn thing. They just ignored everything you told them. But, in fact, they were listening all the time.

A Lesbian Mom

Re-Invents the Extended Family

Susan Stewart, born in 1952 in Bellows Falls, Vermont
Mother of Rhea
Interviewed by Margaret Dragu

MARGARET The first question I ask everybody is the same—when did you first want to have a baby?

SUSAN I wanted to have a baby five years before I had one. I stopped taking birth control, and it looked like I was infertile, because I went five years and no baby—and I had basically given up on the idea of having a baby when I got pregnant. It was a complete surprise.

MARGARET How old were you?

SUSAN Thirty-one. Suddenly I was pregnant and, as it happens to most women, it seemed like totally the wrong time in my life to get pregnant, like it couldn't have been worse—

MARGARET You couldn't wait to have it happen for five years, and then, when you actually were pregnant, it was the wrong time.

SUSAN That's right [*laughs*]—which is totally normal, I think.

MARGARET How did having a child compare to how you thought it would be?

SUSAN It was completely different. I really had a lot of misconceptions. I didn't have any experience with children up until that point. I hadn't had the extended-family experience, but I had fantasies of what it would be like, and one of my fantasies was that I would have my art studio, I would take my child to my studio, my child would play in the play-pen, and I would go in the darkroom and do my work—a vision of continuing as an artist and the child just hanging out with me while I was doing all this [*laughs*], quietly playing in the play-pen. It didn't quite work out like that. It was five years of not doing any of my own work. It was five years out of my life devoted to my child, which I don't regret at all. But it was a shock.

MARGARET And you were the prime care-giver for those first five years?

SUSAN I was in a relationship with the baby's father when I had her and, for the first 18 months, I was at home, although, when Rhea was seven months old, I starting taking part-time work, and Peter was working outside the home six days a week. He was overworked, he had his own business, I never saw him. I spent most of that first year at home alone with her.

MARGARET When you did part-time work, who took care of the baby?

SUSAN I found a woman who was taking children into her home—she had three or four children—for half-days.

MARGARET That was when Rhea was a year and a half?

SUSAN No, I started that when she was seven months, for two or three times a week. Then, when she was 18 months old, I put her in full-time daycare, and I went back to work full-time.

MARGARET When you were working part-time, was that money enough to pay for baby care?

SUSAN It was paying for baby care and some groceries. We were very, very poor the first two years. Peter wasn't bringing home much money, and it was a real struggle economically.

MARGARET So, you had to work to add to the family income.

SUSAN I *had* to work, there was no choice. I also left my relationship at the same time. I started a full-time job, she went into full-time daycare, and Peter and I split up.

MARGARET And you moved! More stress.

SUSAN Oh, terrible stress! I made a bad decision. It was the only decision I could make at the time. Our rent was too high where we were living for me to carry it on my own. So I left the home, and Peter kept the apartment. He got someone else to live with him to share the rent. The next year was one of the hardest years of my entire life. Just going out in the world with a young baby, an 18-month-old child, oh, it was terribly stressful, and I had a series of three apartments in the next year and a half, three living situations, none of them very good

MARGARET What happened when you were on your own?

SUSAN I had to keep moving. A woman was advertising in

the local paper for someone to share her house, and she had a child. I called her. We were two single parents. From the very start, Peter and I did child-sharing. I've always had her for four days, and he had her for three. That was really difficult, too. At 18 months, letting go of her for three days a week, every week, was a tragedy. Every week—incredible anxiety and separation blues. Rhea and I would both be sobbing, to be apart for three days a week. It was horrible, and I was so guilty and stressed out about not being with her a hundred percent of the time.

MARGARET Why did you feel that you should be with her all the time?

SUSAN I had that deep feeling that she needed me, and that I was a bad mother because I wasn't there a hundred percent of the time. It's so complicated, because I realized that I didn't want Peter out of my life, I wanted her to know him, to have a second parent. I didn't leave Peter because I hated Peter. I still loved him, but I was coming into my sexuality as a lesbian before I got pregnant—which is one of the reasons it was a problem for me at that time to get pregnant. I was addressing this as an issue in my relationship with Peter. Having the baby kept Peter and me together longer than we would have gone on together if I hadn't become pregnant.

MARGARET You didn't think that having the baby was not part of your new identity?

SUSAN No, as soon as I knew I was pregnant, I wanted the baby, because I had wanted a child anyway.

MARGARET It was the timing you weren't so sure about, but the idea of becoming a mother was still a good one?

SUSAN Oh, still a good one for me.

MARGARET Did you ever get to meet other lesbian mothers, or were you too busy?

SUSAN What saved my life absolutely was a mothers' support group that I got into very very early on, when Rhea was three or four months old. I realized I needed to talk to other mothers—I didn't know what I was doing, the world, everything seemed crazy to me, I felt totally out of control in my life.

MARGARET There was no grandma around.

SUSAN There was nobody. I have no family around at all within a 3,000-mile radius, they're all out on the East Coast. I had nobody to call, I was also in a new city. I moved to Vancouver when I was five months pregnant, I didn't know very many people at all, I felt completely isolated, and I really felt like I was going out of my mind.

MARGARET I'll bet. I can imagine.

SUSAN It was terrible. So I responded to an ad in *Kinesis,* saying that a feminist mothers' support group was starting. Interested women were to call this number. I instantly called the number—and it was a wonderful woman named Patty Moore. She was working at Vancouver Status of Women. She was a very active feminist, and she had just had a baby nine months before I had Rhea, and she was absolutely going out of her mind.

About five women, all with youngish babies, got together for this support group. I had the support group for two years, we met once a week, and it was my lifeline to sanity.

MARGARET Where did you meet?

SUSAN At each other's houses. We met often at my house. It was a very good group—very feminist and very political. There was a lot of analysis going on about our oppression. [*laughs*] I needed to have that, it was very important for me, because I felt oppressed in my situation, but I didn't know how to articulate it, and I also felt really guilty for feeling this way. I thought I wasn't supposed to have these feelings—everyone else was supposed to be happy and into it—so why was I suffering so much? Why was I coming up with all this stuff? I felt bad, I felt I should be in total joy, or bliss, and I couldn't figure out why I wasn't, why it was such a struggle, why my daily life was such a struggle, and I was really quite unhappy. Although I was totally in love with my child and loved being a mother, the actual reality of my life was very oppressive for lots of different reasons.

MARGARET Can you articulate the reasons?

SUSAN Economically oppressive, being very, very poor. For the first time in my life, I wasn't able to work, because I had to take care of a child, and I've always worked, and suddenly I didn't have my own money. My partner didn't have enough money. We were so poor, and I felt out of control. I was dependent on someone economically, and I was dependent on somebody who couldn't really provide. It was really difficult. I felt oppressed by the sexism in our relationship, in the roles—we fell into these roles. The whole structure of our society puts you in these roles, there is no way around it. You're not living in extended families, there's not a lot of support, and if you're an isolated nuclear family with a man, a woman, and a child, the roles—it's so hard not to fall into them.

MARGARET The Three Bears.

SUSAN Exactly. I was doing all the cooking, I was doing all the laundry, I was doing all the housework, and I was in a role that I didn't like, that I'd been against all my life. That made me feel out of control. I felt very oppressed by it. Then, of course, there was my dream life, in which I was being a lesbian. [*laughs*] And then I was like, Oh god, we'll put that one aside for awhile. My life as an artist had to be put aside, also. These things that were essential in my life were shut down.

MARGARET And you're not allowed to feel angry about that, because that's denying your child.

SUSAN That's right.

MARGARET It becomes either/or. So these other women, the other four women? There were five of you in similar situations?

SUSAN Similar economic and social structure. They had children the same age. Some of them had partners who generated more income—they didn't have *that* stress—but every single one of them had stress in their relationships when the child came in. There wasn't one who didn't have some stuff to go over around that. Some of these women are still with their partners, but for everyone, having a child brought up issues in the relationship. Power dynamics got really sharpened, and suddenly we were all looking at the roles we were put in. It was fantastic to have this group, because it was a place to analyse—and a place to discuss and support.

MARGARET Like-minded people, who have the same values.

SUSAN Yes. We all identified as feminists.

MARGARET Any other lesbians in your group?

SUSAN None of us were lesbians. Now, of that group, two of us are lesbian single moms who child-share with their ex-partners.

MARGARET I started reading Fay Weldon rampantly as soon as Aretha was born. She writes about motherhood. You need someone you can relate to, someone who's had the same experience. Otherwise you'll just keep going crazy. 'Am I the only one who feels like this? What's going on out there, all the brainwashing, the mass media, television? We're all supposed to be enjoying this role, right?' And we're always worried that we're not doing a good enough job.

SUSAN It's an incredible lot of responsibility. I don't know why I don't know anything about this, I don't know why it's such a surprise to me, but I was incredibly shocked by what motherhood did to my life, what it is doing to my life. I haven't caught up with the changes at all.

MARGARET There's an essay by Ursula Le Guin about women writers, the chaos of writing on the corner of the table while the whole extended family goes bananas.

SUSAN Oh, god, I know it.

MARGARET That helped, reading those things, but then it also made me feel, Am I a dolt, or what? I can't get anything done, and I feel so guilty for feeling so miserable and being grumpy, because my own life is gone.

SUSAN Guilt is the key word. We are all so guilty. That's the big one. Everyone's got it. We mothers. We've all got guilt. For one or another reason, we carry around this bundle of guilt.

MARGARET Your mother died when you were quite young.

SUSAN Seventeen, yes. I was young.

MARGARET Did you get some idea of mothering from your mother?

SUSAN When my baby came, for the first time I was able to experience my grief for losing my mother. My life after my mother died, when I was a teenager, was very difficult for a number of years. One of the things I got into was drugs, and I did drugs for 15 years, and I only stopped doing drugs when I got pregnant—I had an incredible addiction. I couldn't stop for myself, but when I got pregnant, I was able to stop. That's the other thing that was going on in my life, I was straight for the first time in 15 years. Which meant the world looked and felt different, and not very pleasant. It was a big crash. That complicated my psychology quite a bit. By doing drugs, I'd suppressed feelings for all those years. That's how the drugs were functioning for me. When I was straight, I had this baby, I had this life.

MARGARET No cushion against the world any more.

SUSAN No cushion. Everything started coming up, including an incredible grief for my mother, which I had suppressed since the day she died. That's the first thing that came up. My mom. I don't know about the parenting, I was an intuitive parent more than anything—I think that expresses how I deal with parenting. I'm not really a perfectionist as a parent. I think, in the spectrum of how parents are described, I'd be considered very liberal, I sort of go with the flow and judge every situation as it comes up and just deal with it.

MARGARET You don't find yourself doing or saying the things that your mother said to you? Unconsciously ...

SUSAN My situation is so different from my mother's. I'm not in a nuclear family, I have a lifestyle that is so completely different, it's almost hard to judge. Rhea's lifestyle is so different than mine as a child.

MARGARET Let's talk about this new lifestyle. What is your day like, what is your week like?

SUSAN It's changed a lot. When she was 18 months old, I started a full-time job at an art gallery, and I had that job for four-and-a-half-years. That was an incredibly difficult, stressful lifestyle. I was commuting, I had a regular, normal, seven-and-a-half-hour day with one hour attached to each end, of driving. It was a nine-and-a-half-hour day away from home. My day was nuts. Totally nuts. I would get up at six in the morning. I would get myself ready for work, pack my lunch, get her ready for daycare, pack a lunch and all that for her, be at the daycare at quarter to eight or 7:30, drop her off that early in the morning with her stuff, say good-bye to her, be gone for nine hours, come back exhausted after driving for an hour in rush-hour traffic, get to the daycare at 5:30, pick her up, be totally, totally wiped out, prepare supper for us, and we'd both be in bed by 8:30 or nine o'clock. Those years were just one state of exhaustion for me, total exhaustion.

MARGARET Peter was there?

SUSAN She spent Thursdays, Fridays, and Saturday nights with Peter. The only thing that saved me was having those three nights off. But that was also hard in a different way. I had to drop her off, and we would always have this incredible weeping, and oh, the separation, and I would be guilty the whole three days, and worrying about her constantly.

MARGARET And guilty leaving her at daycare.

SUSAN Guilty leaving her at daycare. My guilt—capital G guilt, capital U, I, L, T guilt! [*laughs*]

MARGARET Guilt-full.

SUSAN Full tilt. I had four-and-a-half years of the highest stress. I can't imagine doing that to myself again. I don't know how I survived it now, looking back at it.

MARGARET And in the middle of that was your coming-out process?

SUSAN Yes, that's right, I was in a relationship with a woman. We weren't living together, but ... my whole coming-out process was happening.

MARGARET Was there incredible love? Were you in love?

SUSAN It was incredible. I was in love.

MARGARET Surprised, shocked, and ...

SUSAN What I remember most about this relationship—which I am no longer in—is the scheduling fights we had. [*laughs*] I had an incredible work-week with all this time spent and all this guilt, and I had to have time alone with Rhea—that was very, very important—so I had a five-day work-week and Sunday was the day I kept for Rhea, the whole day, and I had to bond in my one day a week with my child, who was only two years old—one day a week—and this was precious. That was my day with Rhea, that was her special day, plus I needed a couple of evenings with her a week alone, one-to-one, I had so little time with her, this was essential. Then there was the time with the lover, and the lover wanted way more time than I was able to give, so the lover got two nights, three nights a week. Two of those with me alone, and one night with me and Rhea. That left one night a week—Thursday night—Thursday is still a special day to me. [*laughs*] Thursday night!

MARGARET So you went to the disco?

SUSAN Are you kidding? Me? I did housework. No, I read and then I went to bed, but I was *alone*, from 5:30 until 9:00 when I went to sleep on Thursday night, I was alone. It was the only time in the whole week that I was alone, and it had such significance. I used to unplug the phone, lock the door.

MARGARET Was it more exciting than having a new relationship with your new girlfriend?

SUSAN My poor dear lover Kate, she suffered being with me for four years. More than a hot love relationship, we were parenting each other in a different kind of way, and I needed her support desperately. And she needed mine for different reasons–what I was able to give her. I wouldn't say this was a mad passionate love affair. This was more survival. On top of all this, I was starting to do my artwork again, I would take time out on Saturdays to work on my art. Not every Saturday, but consistently on Saturdays.

MARGARET That must have been frightening and exhilarating and exciting and scary, thinking, Oh my god, I haven't done it for so long, can I still do it?

SUSAN It was all that.

MARGARET But you were doing art again at last.

SUSAN Right. I was still living apart from Peter. However, about six months after Peter and I split up, he got involved with a woman, a friend of mine actually, who lived in a co-op. When they got together in the co-op, another apartment became available—a bigger one—so they moved into that apartment and their old apartment, the smaller one, came up, and I asked to come into that.

MARGARET You must have had some interesting meetings to work this out.

SUSAN The whole process was very, very interesting. I made a commitment to myself and to Rhea to maintain a friendship with Peter, and a close relationship, because I figure you have two choices when you break up a family. You can either hate each other and have as little to do with each other as possible, or you can try to maintain a relationship and make it a loving and warm one. It takes a lot of work, but that's the choice I made. Down the road, I see it being very beneficial to everybody involved. Because Peter is her father, we would be spending many many years together in terms of co-parenting, one way or another.

MARGARET You had a post-marital relationship.

SUSAN Exactly. Peter and I went into some counselling with the people at Rape Relief and were working out our issues. It was peer counselling, and there were five of us. A male friend of Peter's. A woman friend of mine. And the partner of one of Peter's male friends. Peter was involved in Rape Relief. He was on the men's committee at the time, and Rape Relief has a commitment to helping with interpersonal relationship problems. They see that as a part of their whole mandate, which I really respect, because relationships are a political issue. We got together regularly to meet and discuss the issues of our relationship, and how we were going to work it out, and it was really a good process. It didn't go on for very long, because Peter got involved with Lorraine, and that kind of blew the whole process.

MARGARET Lorraine was part of the peer counselling?

SUSAN No, she was a friend of mine and—

MARGARET That seemed too close?

SUSAN It was too close. That was one of my old issues with Peter. Other involvements. It sabotaged our whole counselling process. That was a very difficult period after that. But I still made a huge effort to carry on a relationship with him.

MARGARET With him and with her?

SUSAN With Lorraine, that was even more problematic. I didn't talk to her for a year. I was very hurt and angry, and it was difficult. When the apartment came up, Lorraine and I hadn't spoken for a solid year, but we got together because we all saw that this was a very interesting solution to the problem of co-parenting.

MARGARET To be physically close helps on co-parenting issues.

SUSAN We're talking houses side by side here—shared backyard and really, really close. We got together, and we had this whole incredible thing where there was all this forgiveness and we resumed a friendship and healed a lot. It was hard work. It was a totally good thing to do, though. All that hard work, all that processing, that difficulty, all that paid off. Now I'm getting the pay-off for it, because we have such a wonderful situation. Peter and Lorraine's family is now like my extended family. It's so nice for me to have that. To be close to this family and to be growing up with all these children in the co-op. Lorraine was a single parent at the time, she has a child. And she and Peter now have a child together, little Rosa, and we share Rhea, and it's like one big family. It's just lovely.

MARGARET You're comfortable with Lorraine as the third parent?

SUSAN Oh yes, she's definitely the third parent. We make decisions together—I think extended families are wonderful. I don't mean everyone has to be related to each other.

MARGARET Non-biological extended families.

SUSAN Non-biological extended families, where a number of adults are sharing responsibility for a number of children. That happened in communities in the past, but now it's this nuclear family thing, everybody's into it, but it's really not the best way, and especially not the best way for me. It's good to share that work. Share the economics as much as possible. What a difference it makes. It's so rewarding in so many ways for me to be part of these other children's lives, something like an aunt. You get a wonderful sense of continuity, a wonderful sense of being part of something bigger than yourself. Our situation is quite unique. Often when families split apart, there's all this pain and suffering and not coming back together.

MARGARET There's all that ripping and trauma.

SUSAN I say, try to heal that wound, and try to see what's on the other side of that—it could be something very, very beautiful. If you can manage it. People split up for different reasons.

MARGARET That's right. It sounds like Peter was very agreeable about working something out. He had certain similar values, enough that you had a chance to work through all the difficult pain and hurt and get on to something. You wouldn't have hooked up with him and had a baby with him if he was a complete bozo.

SUSAN No, he's very progressive. We decided to do nothing legally when we split. We decided to forget that whole idea of going to the courts and doing the custody thing. We did everything by trust and by making verbal agreements with each other, and it takes a lot of faith and trust, but you can build a relationship on faith and trust. That's what we've been doing, building a relationship.

MARGARET Building up a whole new relationship based on the faith and the relationship you had at first.

SUSAN And now it's so wonderful. As soon as I moved into the co-op, I had access to Rhea every day, and Peter does, too, if he wants. She's playing in our same backyard. We share it. Even if she's not staying with me, I see her every day, and for her it's totally integrated. It's the perfect solution.

MARGARET She still spends three days with him and four with you?

SUSAN Yes, Thursday to Saturday she spends the night there. But she can come home any time, because I'm right there. She often comes first thing in the morning to get her shoes which she left the night before. It's back and forth all the time.

MARGARET Perfect.

SUSAN It's very nice.

MARGARET So now Rhea's part of a blended family next door.

SUSAN Yes, and then, of course, my woman lovers come into it, and so she's also getting the experience of a lesbian household.

MARGARET Not all the rest of the kids at school will know about that. [*laughs*]

SUSAN No, that's the other thing. She came home the other day from school. I don't have a television set and—

MARGARET And that's what makes you more unusual.

SUSAN [*laughs*] Right! That makes me more unusual than the fact that I'm a lesbian. She came home from school, and she was the only child in the class who didn't have a television. They were studying TV.

MARGARET We don't have a TV either. It's amazing, what a much bigger issue it is than anything. Tell me, did mothering affect your self-esteem?

SUSAN My sense of self-esteem had taken an incredible dip.

MARGARET You'd better believe it. Everyone bottoms out in the self-esteem department. [*laughs*] Big sale in self-esteem! Going fast! Because you're poor. Therefore you must be stupid.

SUSAN Exactly.

MARGARET You don't have any control of your life. You can't make any decisions, you can't make any changes.

SUSAN Career, what's that? [*laughs*]

MARGARET Art? Huh? For example, I haven't cut my hair since I got pregnant.

SUSAN I can relate to that.

MARGARET For some reason, I'm waiting for something to really change, to feel incredibly empowered before I do that. It's almost mythological. I started doing a kind of Jungian thinking, Oh, I used to be the whore, now I'm the mother, and I can see the crone is coming on really fast. She'll make herbal tinctures, and tell people the northeast wind's coming.

SUSAN [*laughs*] Right.

MARGARET Did you get to meet any other lesbian mothers? Are there any other stresses that come from being that special kind of mom?

SUSAN In Calgary there is a lesbian mothers' support group, a really big one, I don't think there is one in Vancouver. But there are tons and tons of lesbian mothers. That's what's so great about Vancouver, because it's not unusual. I have several friends whom I socialize with regularly who are lesbian mothers, and so, for Rhea, it's really normal, which is fantastic.

MARGARET No TV is going to be a hardship for her, but the lesbian mother—

SUSAN I've talked to lesbians with older children who see the homophobia cropping up among their kid's friends. That's when you have to start dealing with it and explaining. But at age eight, I've not yet had to do that.

MARGARET Well, that's great.

SUSAN I think it's unique to where I'm living. I've chosen a place where there are lots of gays and lesbians. There's a lot of visibility—it's not a whole closeted thing—and there's not a lot of fear about being out. I mean a rural community, forget it. That's a whole separate—

MARGARET High River, Alberta, let's go!

SUSAN Right! You know, this is fun. I like it. I talk about sex and art all the time, but do I ever get to talk about being a mother? Never. This is totally new.

MARGARET How has being a mom changed your art? Not just the process of making art, but the actual art itself?

SUSAN One of my regrets—and it's nothing that I could control—is that I couldn't make art while I had a young baby. What I would've said in my artwork then would've been very different than at absolutely any other time in my life—because the experience of being and the feelings I was having towards children, towards babies, was very intense. Because I had no time and no money, I wasn't able to practice art during that period, which is a real shame. I felt very motivated to do art even when I had her, without any possibility of doing it. There is a lot I would have said about the experience that I never got to say. I made one poster, and I used her in it, and it's quite swell, but that's all I managed. [*laughs*]

MARGARET Motherhood doesn't inform your work in a major way at the moment?

SUSAN It informs my work in the sense that the emotional depth that I bring to anything now is so different than before I had her. Having a child is the most amazing teacher. For me it was the most amazing teacher in the world, in my life.

MARGARET What did it teach you specifically?

SUSAN A lot about love, and it taught me a lot about devotion. And commitment. As a parent, as a mother of a young baby, you devote yourself entirely to another being, and I had never done that before. That is a path. Any mother can tell you, any mother knows it. Devoting that much of your time, 24 hours a day, over so many years, to one other being and putting yourself to the side, it gives you incredible spiritual depth that you don't have before that process. Any work I do now is informed with this new knowledge, and this new understanding—what it means to be a woman and a parent and a mother. An understanding of the continuity of life. All this is deep, deep stuff, that I learned from this process. So yes, hopefully that informs my work.

MARGARET *Je ne regrette rien.*

SUSAN Boy, did I ever wax philosophic there. [*laughs*]

MARGARET It's amazing, the big words I use when I try to describe motherhood—it always sounds like I took them from a greeting card. I just put those words in my vocabulary now, and they weren't there before.

SUSAN Yes, exactly.

MARGARET Although, sometimes, I'm bitterly resentful about the sleep deprivation and years of putting all our own needs on hold.

SUSAN It shouldn't be that hard. It's our social system that makes it that hard. It could be a lot easier. You could experience all the good things and maybe not so many of the really difficult things that we have to experience because of the social conditions of being a mom.

MARGARET You were politicized before you became a mother, but this must have really clinched it.

SUSAN It politicized me around motherhood, which I didn't have before. I look back on how I was with mothers—naive and unconscious. The personal is political, that old line.

MARGARET That old line, it's a good tune.

Breaking the Maternal Silence

No More *Good* Mothers

Susan Swan, born in 1945 in Midland, Ontario
Mother of Samantha
Interviewed by Sarah Sheard

SUSAN I am a novelist, and my daughter was the beginning of my artistic life.

SARAH When did you first want to have a baby?

SUSAN It was never very clear in my mind. I thought I would have a child the way I thought about graduating from college: Some day I'd graduate from college and get a job, I'd grow up and have a baby, but I wasn't sure how that was going to happen. I had a very traditional mother who worked very hard for the family and, I thought, had to be very selfless, and I used to think, some day I will have to be really selfless, too, but for the time being, I might as well be as selfish as I can. It wasn't a clear thing. Then I got married, and my marriage started to fail, and I suspect I got pregnant thinking it would save the marriage, when it was actually going to save me—but I didn't know that then.

SARAH How old was Sam when your marriage ended?

SUSAN Samantha was 10 months old when my marriage ended. I'd been married for four years, and had been seeing her father for four years before that, and I knew when I was pregnant that there was a good chance that the marriage wasn't going to work out—so I had a great joy and pleasure in the sensuality of pregnancy, but at the same time, terror and sadness about what was to come, because I suspected that I'd have to make my way on my own, which indeed I did.

SARAH It came to you before you had even given birth, that your marriage was coming to an end?

SUSAN It did, and it didn't. I went back and forth. I would have moments of clarity where I'd think, No, it's not going to work, and then my hope would start again, that it would work. For a short time after Samantha was born, our marriage was better. The birth was such a triumphant moment. I hadn't been prepared for the feeling of accomplishment that went with having a baby. I was addicted then to traditional masculine values, to a masculine notion of what accomplishment meant. The idea of the woman getting fulfilment from doing something that was a natural thing for her to do seemed corny to me, but when I did give birth, I felt triumphant. I felt like the greatest warrior in the world. I just exalted in it, and for a short time the birth did bring my ex-husband and me together, but it wasn't enough to carry the marriage.

SARAH He shared in that exaltation? You didn't became mother and therefore an untouchable object to him? Or am I prying?

SUSAN Oh, you can pry. When I became a mother, my ex-husband still saw me as a romantic figure. He didn't see me as an asexual mother. Having a baby was an accomplishment for him, too. He was there at the birth, and although he developed a habit of sleeping very soundly shortly after the baby was born—he had been a light sleeper before she came—he participated a great deal, and I didn't get any sense of change in his perception of me. I certainly felt changed in my understanding of what the passing of time means and who I am. You see, I realized when I had a child that I was going to die, and I didn't know that before. I'd always thought I was going to live forever, and the writing I wanted to do would be accomplished some day in the future. When Samantha arrived, I realized I'd better get at it, because my time was finite. I also used the baby as a good way of saying no, which I had not really been able to do before.

SARAH To say no sexually or in terms of social obligations?

SUSAN Not sexually, but in terms of people making demands on me. I used to feel obliged to fulfil other people's fantasies, but once I had a child, I realized that I could no longer do that, because I wouldn't be able to look after the baby. It was also the beginning of the period in my life when I started to assert myself. I began to write fiction and poetry, which I'd always wanted to do, and within two years of her birth, I'd put on my first performance piece, a play about my love-hate relationship with the figure-skater Barbara Ann Scott.

SARAH It is interesting to see how often the assertion of self also signals the beginning of the end of the relationship that you have had with a man.

SUSAN Yes. It did mean, in my case, that I gained a child and lost a husband—but I think I was going to lose that husband anyway. We had a difference in values and goals that was becoming clearer and clearer. In terms of my own life, it felt like a child taught me structure. I hadn't known how to create structure for myself, but once I had a kid who I was literally psychically and physically chained to, I had to devise and retain a structure that did give me some time to do some writing and time to look after her, and this was new, because I used to work very hard, but I never approached it in any systematic way.

SARAH Is this what you are referring to when you talk about your daughter's birth being the start of your creative life?

SUSAN Yes. In the 10 years after she was born, I wrote two books of fiction, and numerous performance and journalism pieces. Being pregnant was the start of taking my own aspirations seriously—but I am telling you now all the good things about being a mother, and avoiding the bad, like our mothers who kept the dark side of the experience secret. I am telling you that it taught me how to stand up for myself and build structure, and it also gave me a sense that I had a responsibility to myself and my work, but I am leaving out the other, more terrible part. You see, it helped me to be more definite about what I wanted to do—but a terrible, paralysing guilt and sense of powerlessness went with being a mother and a writer.

When I was working on a book, I felt like I was taking away time from Samantha, and I had no role models at that time of women who had successfully juggled those two things, and it seemed like I could not—I could not get it right. Either my work was suffering, or the child was suffering. I've read studies that suggest that women writers see their work as conflicting with, or substituting for, biological children. For instance, Marilyn Yalom, in her book *Maternity, Morality, and the Literature of Madness*, talks about the French writer Emma Santos, who perceived a stillborn child as the price she was paying for working hard on a book. I saw the two things in opposition, too—and they were. Now that Samantha is 18, I can see that she wasn't really deprived. The time that I was putting into my work did not hurt her, but it certainly was not something that she always liked me to do. I remember once locking myself into a car to finish a short story, and looking up to see Samantha and a friend pressing their faces against the car windshield. It was hard to insist on time to work, and I'm sure child care cut into my literary output.

SARAH Were there any times in which the creative inspiration and the experience of motherhood came together? In other words, did you ever find yourself writing about the actual experience of having a child, or being a mother?

SUSAN Interesting, because what I did again was to deny in some way the real-time and real-life situation I was in. I used to feel impatient with myself, that I had not got the times spent looking after Samantha better organized, and I saw that time as somethingthat I did incidentally to the rest of my working day.

SARAH Yes.

SUSAN I didn't get any child-support from my ex-husband until Samantha was eight. I supported myself and Samantha. We were living in a co-op. I was writing fiction and looking after her, and I really didn't give myself any credit for the time I put into her. I thought that it was something that I should just accomplish effortlessly and, of course, that's laughable when you think about it. I denied the experience of motherhood in some ways as I was going through it. I very much reflected the attitudes of the culture at that time—I would take jobs to make money, and my employers would act as if they didn't know I was a working mother with a child. In the business world, children didn't exist, and I didn't question this much.

SARAH How did you deal with the issue of money? Money is obviously an issue for a single parent raising a child.

SUSAN Yes. It was compounded, in my case, because I wanted to write fiction, and that made it harder financially, because I not only needed to make money for my daughter and myself, I needed to make money to buy myself time to write. But that was my personal choice. The situation of being a mother and having to make money is part of a horrible scam that you are suddenly parachuted into when you give birth—you have no idea about the extent of the problems until it happens. You need to pay the baby-sitter so that you can work to make money, and the baby-sitter costs money. My own mother helped me with baby-sitting, and I also had daycare subsidy when Samantha was two years old, but as soon as I started to make a bit more money at my job, then I no longer qualified for daycare subsidy, and I would end up making slightly less money by the time I paid the baby-sitter. It seemed, when she was very small, that I was on an awful treadmill.

I am an educated woman, I have more options than a lot of women in our society, and I used to go down to the daycare subsidy office and see the women sitting there, looking very subdued, as if having no money was their fault—they were doing a job nobody values, and they were asking for money, and they felt guilty. It was unhealthy that they had to ask for money, and that used to make me really mad, and once I did lose my temper in the office, and suddenly all the women jumped up and got mad too, and ran around, and I thought then, I should organize a protest and do political work, but I was usually too exhausted to do something like that. I decided that I would write about it at some point. I still haven't.

Charlotte Whitton, a former mayor of Ottawa, once said that for a woman to succeed at a job, she had to be twice as good as a man. 'Luckily,' she added, 'that isn't hard.' I still chuckle over that remark, but I think she underestimated things a bit. She didn't take having children into account. I was quite schizophrenic about raising a child and doing my writing, and very unhappy. The idea of this being a source of inspiration for my work was not in the cards back then. A few poems about children dribbled in, but mothering as a major subject—I hadn't come to terms with it.

SARAH Have you writen about that experience?

SUSAN No, I haven't, and I am not sure why that is. It may be that, because I was a single parent, I've had a lot of work backed up in me that would have got expressed earlier if I hadn't been so engaged with child-raising. Or, perhaps it's just taken time for me to digest the experience, because there wasn't anything around me as I was going through it that reflected my feelings. My emotional reactions and experience as a mother were a really dark secret. I felt, for instance, constantly unacknowledged, constantly in a state of rage about the powerlessness of being a mother. I felt furious with men, because they didn't have to go through this. They didn't know what I was going through. Motherhood is the most under-paid, under-acknowledged, and over-sentimentalized job in the world.

SARAH What about the images of mothering as an adventure in literature and culture? As kids, we read the adventure stories of boys and girls. For instance, the C.S. Lewis books and the Enid Blyton books—about adventurous British kids who had no mother to speak of. We don't grow up with literary images of mothers and their relationship to kids. We rarely see positive images of women as mothers in literature.

SUSAN There was an image of mothering in popular culture that was an imprisoning model of femininity. That is the mother who never lost her temper. Like the mother in the TV show 'Father Knows Best.' She was constantly cheerful and looking after the needs of the other people in the family. But the mother who went on adventures with children, she didn't exist, that I can recall. A stigmatizing notion of selfishness was attached to the woman who stepped outside this role. Women are always accused of being selfish when they are simply being self-interested. There is no distinction made here, so the mother who didn't play that traditional role was immediately castigated as a selfish mom. We needed more self-interested moms in our literature and our films, but we didn't have them.

SARAH When you reflect on your childhood, can you think of any mothers who were, in fact, self-interested mothers? Who were living lives in which they were taking charge of their own needs as well as those of their children?

SUSAN Sarah, I can't think of one.

SARAH I rest my case, ladies and gentlemen of the jury. How did motherhood differ from your expectations?

SUSAN I didn't realize having a child was such a primal experience. You co-exist with another individual's emotional needs at such close quarters. This small, unformed individual's first interest is to get you to enter their emotional reality. My daughter was very good at getting me to do that. I sometimes felt I lived at a primitive emotional level with her— like I was creeping around the floor of some bizarre post-Freudian jungle.

I was being buried alive under Barbie dolls and unwashed dishes, and although I could beat my chest, it was always very physically tiring and emotionally draining. I knew that, as an adult, my job was to try to take the experience from that level to something more tempered—so my perspective could guide the child rather than be overwhelmed by the child's drives and needs, which I felt and identified with very strongly.

I also didn't like having so much authority. It was very frightening to me. I felt like I was going to misuse it, and I remember once getting very, very angry with my daughter. I was just exhausted at the end of the day, and she turned to me, and she said, after I had blown my top, she said, 'Mom, I am only a little girl.' I thought, Yes, that's right—and she seemed quite often to be reminding me of the difference in our perspectives and experiences. She was a formidable opponent at times, in terms of her grown-up will and her ability to undermine and unstick me, so I could forget she was only a child.

SARAH Children do have an incredible power over one, don't they?

SUSAN They sure do. That was one of the most shocking things about being a mother. I had assumed they would be more malleable—and I suppose more intimidated—by one as an adult. Yet my daughter's personality was always extremely strong. Freud makes this point about children's passions being full-scale adult passions that just happen to be housed in little bodies—and that's really true. You have your work cut out for you if you are trying to guide and direct a child.

I had an image of how I should be, and then I'd find myself reduced to the level of a child. My mother was a very kind mother and a very patient mother, and I don't remember her ever being angry with us, although I know she was very frustrated and had her problems, but it wasn't something that she aired with her friends or, certainly, talked about with us. Although I really knew her experience had been more complex than she'd presented it, I still had enough vested in her as a good mother that I didn't believe she had problems. When I was not what I thought the good mother was, I felt the most failed I have ever felt.

SARAH So you tried to match her equanimity, and found yourself falling short of that from time to time, but then expressing your frustration and anger in the ways that she never had or maybe never could.

SUSAN Yes, it was a terrible conflict, and the other temper tantrum that I remember of mine—notice I say of mine and not my daughter's—was witnessed by my ex-boyfriend and his small son. They saw me blow up at my daughter, and it was as if all of them had seen the Wicked Witch of the West. My old boyfriend gently took me aside and walked me into another room and got me a cup of tea and never mentioned it again. It was as if it had not happened. He had his problems as a parent, too, but he had a nanny to help with his child-raising, so I don't know if he fully understood the day-to-day fatigue that I experienced with child-raising. He was also a single parent.

I used to feel deeply ashamed—embarrassed and mortified—when I behaved angrily. It wasn't until much later that I realized, getting angry in front of a child isn't the worst thing that could happen. In fact, my daughter and I were in Greece two summers ago, and we were on a very crowded bus, and I got very mad at the bus driver and started to yell at him, and she just laughed and said, 'I am going to turn up my Sony Walkman now, mom.' Somewhere along the way, she's learned that when somebody gets mad, it isn't the end of the world—but certainly I thought it was, that I should be burned at the stake for it.

SARAH Because you're a writer, and because you are who you are, you have a need for a tremendous amount of privacy in your life. Of course, the child works to unravel your desire for privacy, and is at odds for quite a few years with this need. How did you deal with that?

SUSAN That is the most uncanny thing, because I used to notice that as long as I was doing a task that involved my hands, my daughter was perfectly happy to play by herself. For instance, if I was cooking, drawing, sewing—or doing any sort of domestic task—she went about her business, but once I sat at the table and began to write or talk on the phone, it was very threatening to her. She would try to intercede between me and my thoughts, and I used to find that desperate-making. Then I figured out this must be a survival mechanism children have—because if the mother is distracted, it could be life-threatening.

SARAH Yes.

SUSAN I couldn't understand why she couldn't understand this, and I would explain it and explain it and explain, it but it was something that she didn't understand. So what I used to do was to work outside our house. I needed to have a room outside my domestic situation.

SARAH A studio space which you could go to?

SUSAN Yes. Then I didn't have to be constantly resurrecting the boundaries that she had penetrated. They were already in place, and I could just remove myself and put myself in that environment.

SARAH Did you find it difficult to turn off your mother-monitor when you started to sink into your own work and your own mind? Did you find some part of you remained a monitor of Samantha's activities and well-being?

SUSAN Yes, I was always conscious of how much time was going by. I never had the sense of being able to lose myself in time. That was a luxury I didn't have as a writer then. I had to be back in time for the baby-sitter. If I was working in the home and she was there, and she and the baby-sitter didn't seem to be getting along, I sensed that, and it immediately would cut into my concentration. That was why I finally hit upon working at my writing outside the home—for me it was the best solution. But that's more expensive, and that's not always an option for mothers who write or work when their children are around them.

SARAH How do you spend your day?

SUSAN Now, it seems pure luxury, because my daughter is virtually grown up, and she has been living with her father for the last couple of years, so we travel together on our holidays. We usually take a trip somewhere together, and we are travelling companions, and there isn't any child-care obligation.

SARAH Tell me about disciplining your child.

SUSAN Oh, discipline—what a nightmare. The first thing about discipline is that I was under the mistaken impression that you told a child something once, and you never had to tell the child again—I was so impressed with their emotional power that I granted them intellectual reasoning to go with it. Which, of course, they don't have. I used to be constantly astonished and frustrated, and even insulted, that Samantha didn't seem to take in the instructions that I carefully laid out for her, or was once again trespassing on boundaries I'd set up, or ignoring some rule that I'd made.

When she was small, I made a decision not to spank her, and I used to say that she would have to go to her room if she hadn't done what I wanted her to do. This was usually punctuated by requests for glasses of water, et cetera, and I'd get worn down, and it never felt really clean. Discipline always felt very messily executed. I used to envy my old boyfriend's discipline methods, although he seemed a little fierce to me. He could be very tough with his son. For instance, he had a joke. He used to say to his son, 'When I say jump, what do you say?' and the son would say, 'How high?' and we'd all laugh, ha ha. But it wasn't totally a joke. I don't believe in that kind of traditional approach—it's too much like a military model, no matter how much you make fun of it. However, I didn't really have any methodology or philosophy to fill the gap, other than a sense of well-intentioned kindliness.

Going to bed was always an awful time of day, because my daughter and I had a whole ritual that we went through that went on and on for several hours. By the time I got to bed myself, I would be exhausted and overcome and feeling sorry for myself about how she didn't appreciate my patience. I'd just get settled into bed, and then there would be another request for a glass of water or a back rub. When she found out that I could give back rubs, that became a part of it, too. Now, if I'd had more children, I would never ever treat discipline in matters like going to bed in, dare I say, that amateurish way. I would be much more conscious of my rights, but I didn't have any sense of that, because I was still tied to the old-style-mother model.

Eventually, I decided that what I needed was a course in disciplining children, so I read a book, *Children: The Challenge* by Rudolf Dreikurs and Vicki Stolz. An Adult Education Centre at the Toronto Board of Education was giving a course on this book, I went up and took a course for six weeks. The thesis of the book is, essentially, that children learn by experiencing the consequences of their behaviour. Rather than lecture or nag them or over-explain, parents are supposed to set down some ground rules. If your children don't follow these rules, they have to experience the consequences. For instance, if they don't get dressed properly for school, you let them go to school half-dressed. The consequence was the punishment, and it wasn't freighted with morality—that the child had been a bad person because she didn't obey you. It was just a practical thing.

When I began to do this, at first I thought, Oh good, I've got a handle on all this now. However, my daughter quickly learned not to take the consequences too seriously. She'd say, 'Well I know there will be a consequence, but frankly, mom, I don't care,' and she also picked up on the fact that I was approaching it in a mannered way.

SARAH She read that book while you were asleep, right?

SUSAN Yes, and she sensed somehow that there was something rather artificial about me using that construct. It was like importing something, the way you import silk from China, rather than the idea and practice coming out of me. Although the book gave me an ideal, it didn't often become real, because Sam made it part of a game. To tell you the truth, I honestly don't know how I did really discipline her. It seemed that she became more rational and somehow was alert to what was in her best interest. No methodology ever really did the trick. I always respected her as a person and was conscious of her rights, to a fault at times—I wasn't conscious enough of my own rights—and perhaps that eventually paid off, but it didn't feel like it was paying off at the time that we were going through it. I felt victimized.

SARAH The kinds of procedures that are described in *Children: The Challenge* are focused on dealing with younger children. When they reach teenhood, it gets a little bit more complex. Did you find there were specific things, new or different things, that you ran into during the terrible teens?

SUSAN The terrible teens, oddly enough, haven't been that terrible. In fact, they've been pretty calm. The beginning was difficult, when Samantha was about 12 or 13, because she went through a period where she wanted to reject me, and essentially she did do that. She went and lived with her father around this time, and he was much more strict than I, and I couldn't understand why she wanted to live with him—but she did, and I had to accept this.

SARAH If your daughter decided to, say, hook up with a dangerous demon lover, how would you choose to handle that?

SUSAN I would sit down with her and talk over what she was going to get out of it, and whether there were other things that would give her the same thing. I'd ask her whether taking such a step would cut her off from her friends and family, and some of the work that she wants to do. I would see it as a situation where she would have to make the decision herself, after we'd looked at it. She is almost an adult. She was 18 in July. I don't really think, short of her jumping off the Bloor-Danforth Bridge, that I can stop her from doing anything now. She's had a job, she's made some money, so she could arrange it if she wanted to do it.

SARAH You spoke earlier about the role of motherhood being the most unsung, misrepresented, and under-valued role in our society. Do you want to talk a bit more about that?

SUSAN Yes, it has been a very well-kept secret, that men and, unfortunately, women have kept from each other. There's been so much invested in women being good mothers, that to break trust with being a good mother is to admit that you are a failure as a female. I think women have been frightened to really reveal the darker emotions that have gone with mothering—about their frustrations, their sense of anger, their sense of powerlessness. They fear they'll be judged as failures, and it often seems, too, that to assert some of these emotions and feelings—just to bring them out into the open—would somehow be threatening to their own children, and women have been raised to put the needs of their children first.

There hasn't been a way, until recently, for women to talk about this experience without someone construing it as either a threat to their kids' well-being or a failure of personhood in general. This is an outrage. It doesn't help women be better parents to pretend that mothering is one fulfilling moment after another—it's a frustrating job that women are entitled to complain about from time to time.

Men don't really understand, unless they experience it, too. I think there has been a change. Men are more involved in being parents than they ever were in my parents' generation, so this knowledge is becoming a shared knowledge. Before it was really a privileged knowledge that women had but were too frightened—and too intimidated and overworked and under-valued—to admit the truth of what was going on. This is a very sad thing. I often wonder, if women were truly recognized for the contribution they make, whether all our societies would be much healthier places.

SARAH Will you be able to share with Samantha, not only the joy of motherhood, but the pain and discomfort of pregnancy and childbirth and raising a child? She may be like many others, of even our generation, raising a child on her own as well.

SUSAN It's true that's a possibility. I confess, when she asked me if childbirth hurts, I began to feel anxious.

SARAH Yes.

SUSAN Right away. It hurts so much, you think you are going to die, and then I think, I can't tell her that, because that will set in motion a fear she'll have with her until she has a child. It becomes tricky. I usually say that it does hurt an awful lot. I couch it in terms of what you can do to make the hurt seem more natural, but it is probably an unanswerable question. Mothering is never going to be a snap. I think it may always bring up dark dark feelings. It's going to bring up some resentments about the children encroaching on your time. It will bring up feelings of anger you had about the way your parents treated you. It's complicated, and it's never going to be simple, but the fact that it is complex is something we haven't until recently begun to discuss or to acknowledge to one another.

SARAH Your daughter's generation may be the first to really break faith with this maternal conspiracy of silence. Hopefully, it will allow Samantha to share, with her generation of young women having children, the knowledge of motherhood she's gained from you. It could cut the difficulties in half, just being able to share this knowledge.

SUSAN It will certainly cut the difficulties down. There won't be a disavowal of women's actual experience. My daughter and her friends won't have to bump their heads against that brick wall. They will have to contend with the issue of how, as a female, you choose to be a mother—because the way you tackle being a mother also involves how you think of yourself as an individual, and your values. There are always going to be high stakes in mothering—high stakes in terms of personhood—I'm not sure how we can really avoid that. Mothering will be just part of being human. It will be part of the struggle we have to be human and fulfil ourselves. That's a natural struggle as opposed to a kind of struggle where you have an idealized image of a mother to contend with: a good mother does not do this, a good mother is always good, a good mother puts her children first—I think that bogeywoman may be put to bed.

SARAH How would you feel if Samantha were to say to you that she would not ever have a child herself? That she would opt out of that.

SUSAN I don't know, Sarah, because at this point she seems to think having children is one of the greatest joys of life. She's confided to me several times how she's noticed that women who don't have children don't seem to be as flexible or as interesting as the ones who have children. Being a mother is something she really is looking forward to doing, although she says I tried to do everything at once, and that is hard on the mother and the child. She has decided she won't have children until she's in her thirties, and her work or career is established. Recently, a boyfriend of hers said something about how he wasn't going to get up in the night and change his baby's diapers, and my daughter said, 'Well, who will have a baby with you then?' She just took it for granted that a man would participate, and I did not. It always surprises me that she has this positive attitude, that having children is one of the most positive ways you can fulfil yourself, which I admit I did not have. I saw it as something that was unavoidable and a duty—an unavoidable martyrdom.

SARAH Do you ever get womb attacks where you desperately crave another child?

SUSAN Oh yes, yes, I have. I just saw a fortune teller a couple of weeks ago who told me that I have a possibility of two more babies, because I am extremely healthy for a woman of 46. She said that I could do it if I wanted to—and something about the prospect of having more babies is deeply thrilling, but I know what looking after a toddler is like so—

SARAH So, we're crazy. Well, it was just a question. Just a tester. Ready to go back into that breeding barn?

SUSAN Well, not in this lifetime, Sarah.

Editors for the Press: Sarah Sheard and Susan Swan
Cover Design: Brenda Lavoie / Reactor
Printed in Canada

Coach House Press
401 (rear) Huron Street
Toronto, Canada M5S 2G5

A KIND O
RUB THE OXTAILS
PASTE AND CRUSHED BLACK
AND GARLIC, roast at 350 degre
till brown ... Drain...
Simmer oxtails, onions, celery,
pepper, carrots, potatoes, can
tomatoes, cumin, corriander,
pepper or two, oregano, bas
marjoram and
; with r
A das
and water
BE CAREFUL OF TH
The thin,
No 1444
MATRICARIA
TEETHING POWDERS
A Vegetable and Harmless Preparation for Infants.
For Teething, Fretfulness, Catarrh, Restlessness, Feverishness, Rash from Teething, Diarrhœa, Biliousness. Ver
carefully and accurately prepared, and may be given to
most delicate child, more particularly where convu
are feared.
IN BOXES 13, 29, and 46 each, post free.
Prepared by
KEENE & ASHWELL, Limite
The first Homœopathic Chemists in Great Britain,
New Bond Street, Londo
Válido unic
en el Boleto.
ALL BABIES
LIKE I
INSTANTLY STOP
SICKNESS,
FLATULENCE
AND PAIN.
OF GREAT VAL
DIARRHC
IMITATIONS
REFUSE
by Chemists, Grocers, Stores, 1s. 1½d.
's of Infants & Youn
PEELED
TOMATOES
28 fl oz
796 ml
PRODUCT OF ITALY
PRODUIT D'ITALIE
GRIPE WA
DOCTORS
ORDER IT.
BEST,
TAIN
BÉBÉ SOAP
THE BLANCHE LEIGH BÉBÉ SOAP
Especially prepared for the delicate skins of young children and infants.
Price 1 2 per tablet or 3 - per box of 3 tablets.
To be obtained of all Chemists and Stores
Madame BLANCHE LEIGH, 126, Oxford
MENTION THIS PAPER
You should use Blanche Leigh Soap
Nurse says its the best
Molly
Mothers
and
Nurses
should
ask
for
otatoes,
corr
oregan

All day lon
THE OXTAILS WITH TOMATOE
TE AND
PEPPER
GARLIC
grees
POMIDORO PELATI
POMIDORO PELATI
l br
Drain...
mer
gre
per,
of
atoes
per
joram
elvet
OL
hou
"GRIPE WATER."
DOCTORS ORDER IT.
SAFEST, BEST, MOST CERTAIN REMEDY.
ENSURES EASY TEETHING.
PROMOTES DIGESTION.
PREVENTS CONVULSIONS.
ESTABLISHES THE CONSTITUTION.
ALL BABIES LIKE IT.
INSTANTLY STOPS SICKNESS, FLATULENCE AND PAIN.
OF GREAT VALUE IN DIARRHŒA.
IMITATIONS ARE INJURIOUS.
REFUSE ALL SUBSTITUTES.
For all Disorders of Infants & Young Children.
BE CAREFUL OF THE BABY'S SKIN.
sensitive skin of an inf
BABY
SOAP
VINOLIA BABY SOAP
is the blandest and mildest that
be made, and has been specially pr
the tender ski
fonts.
6d.
Ltd., MALDEN